Real World

Colouring Book

For Advanced Users & Adults

50 Images

Created From Real Life Photos
For You To Colour As You Please.

ISBN 978-0-359-79752-3
90000

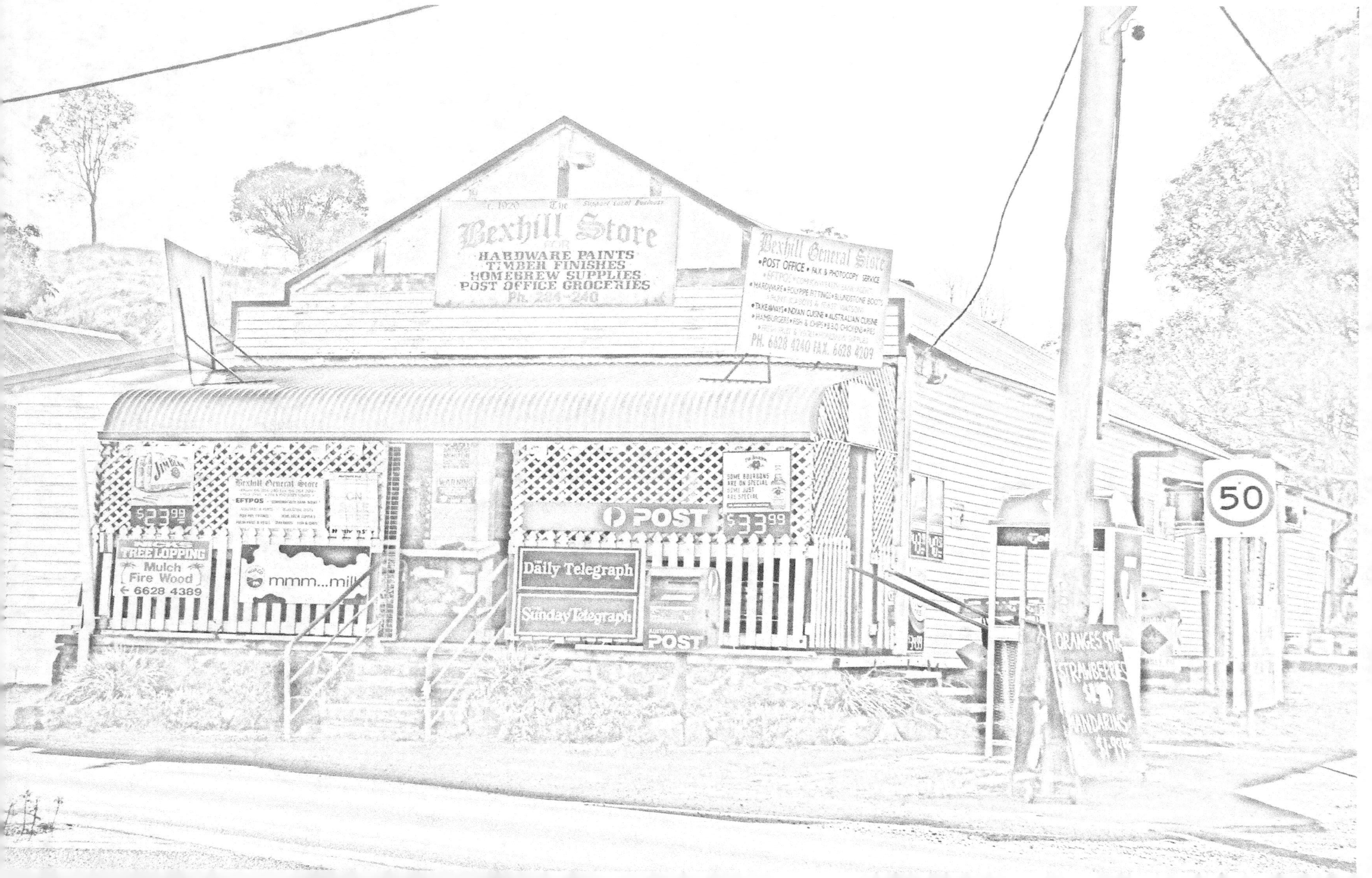
Bexhill Store
HARDWARE PAINTS
TIMBER FINISHES
HOMEBREW SUPPLIES
POST OFFICE GROCERIES
Bexhill General Store
POST OFFICE • FAX & PHOTOCOPY SERVICE
HARDWARE • POLYPIPE FITTINGS • BLUNDSTONE BOOTS
TAKEAWAYS • INDIAN CUISINE • AUSTRALIAN CUISINE
HAMBURGERS • FISH & CHIPS • B.B.Q. CHICKENS • PIES
PH. 6628 4240 FAX. 6628 4209
POST
$33.99
$23.99
TREE LOPPING
Mulch
Fire Wood
6628 4389
mmm...mil
EFTPOS
SOME BOURBONS ARE ON SPECIAL
Daily Telegraph
Sunday Telegraph
POST
50
ORANGES
STRAWBERRIES
MANDARINS

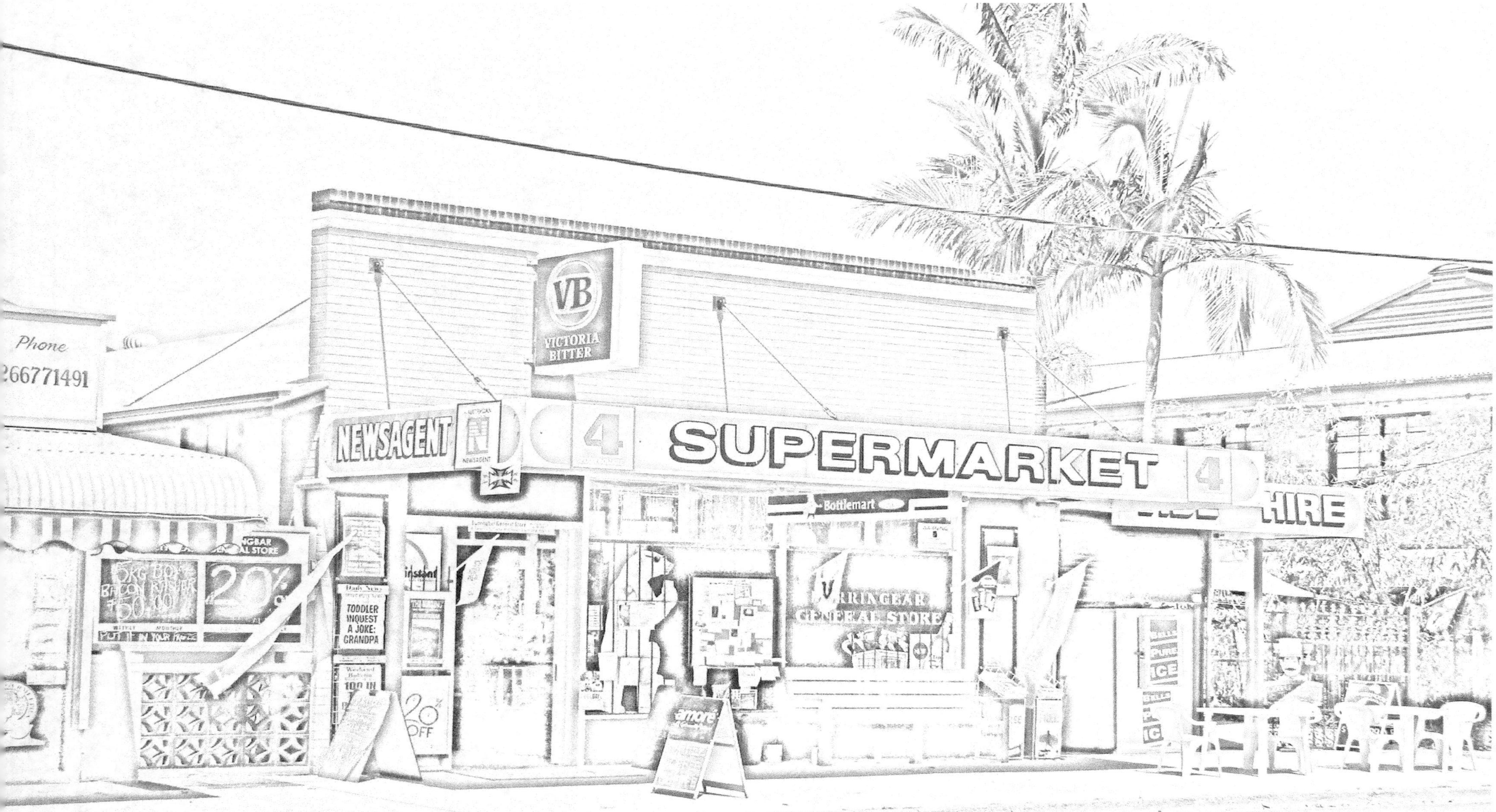
Phone
266771491
VB
VICTORIA BITTER
NEWSAGENT
4
SUPERMARKET
4
HIRE
Bottlemart
GENERAL STORE
TODDLER INQUEST A JOKE: GRANDPA
20% OFF
ICE

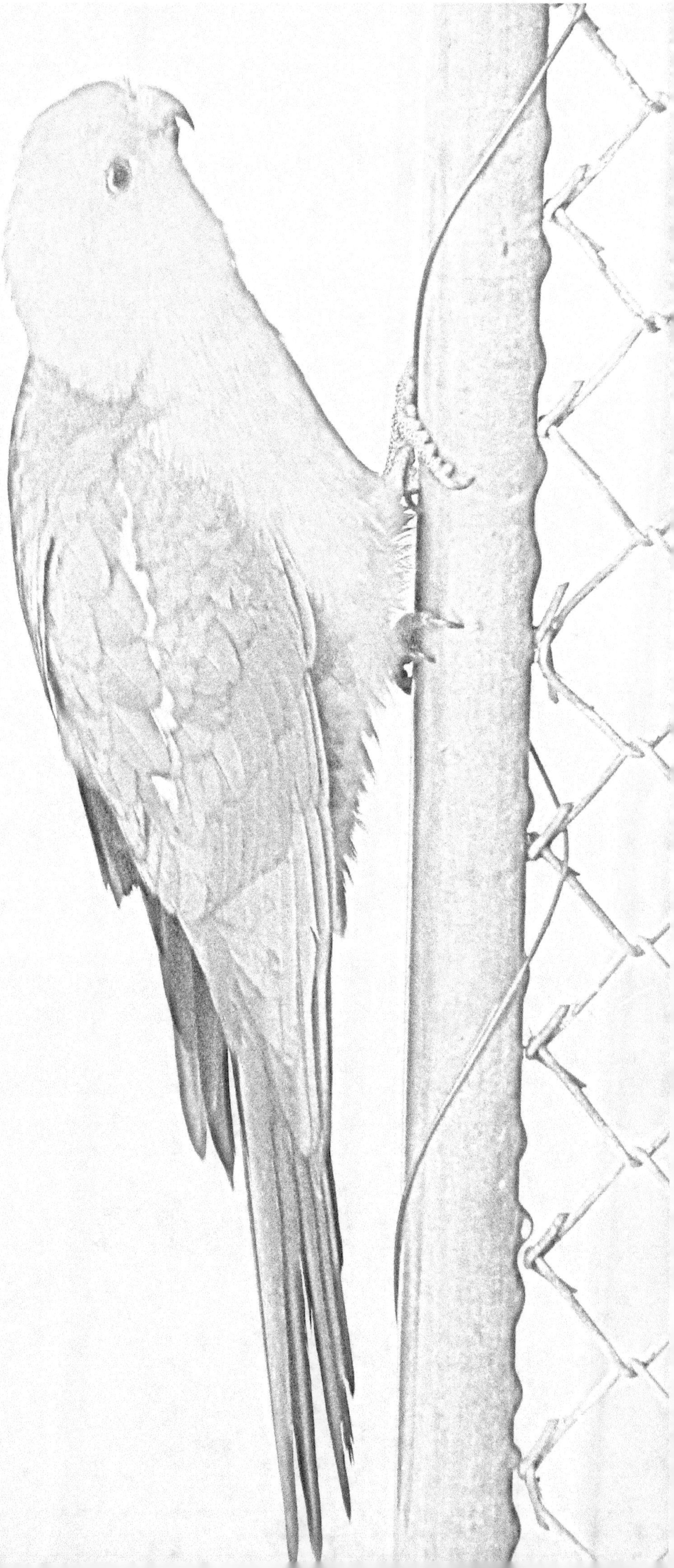

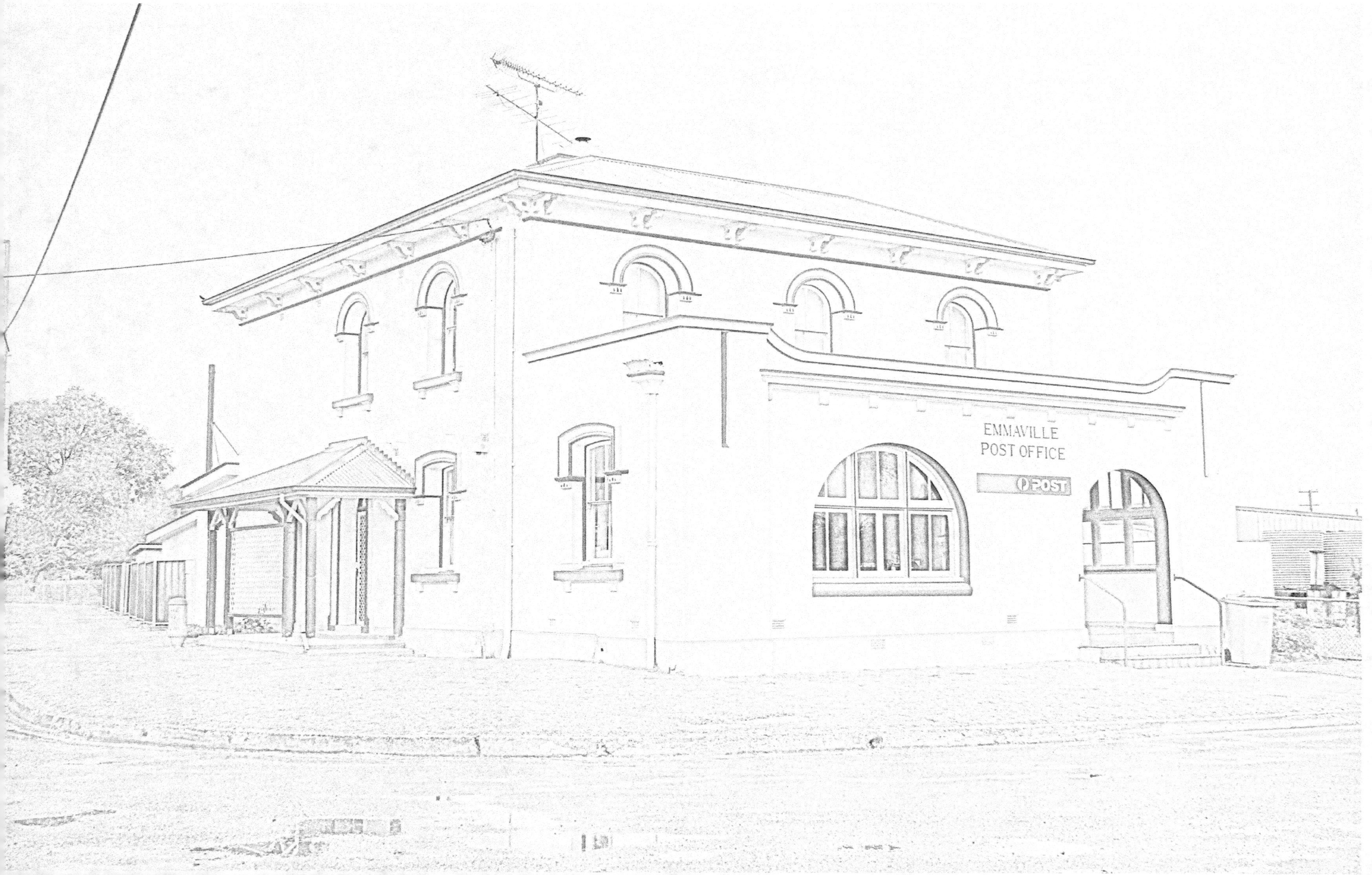
EMMAVILLE
POST OFFICE
POST

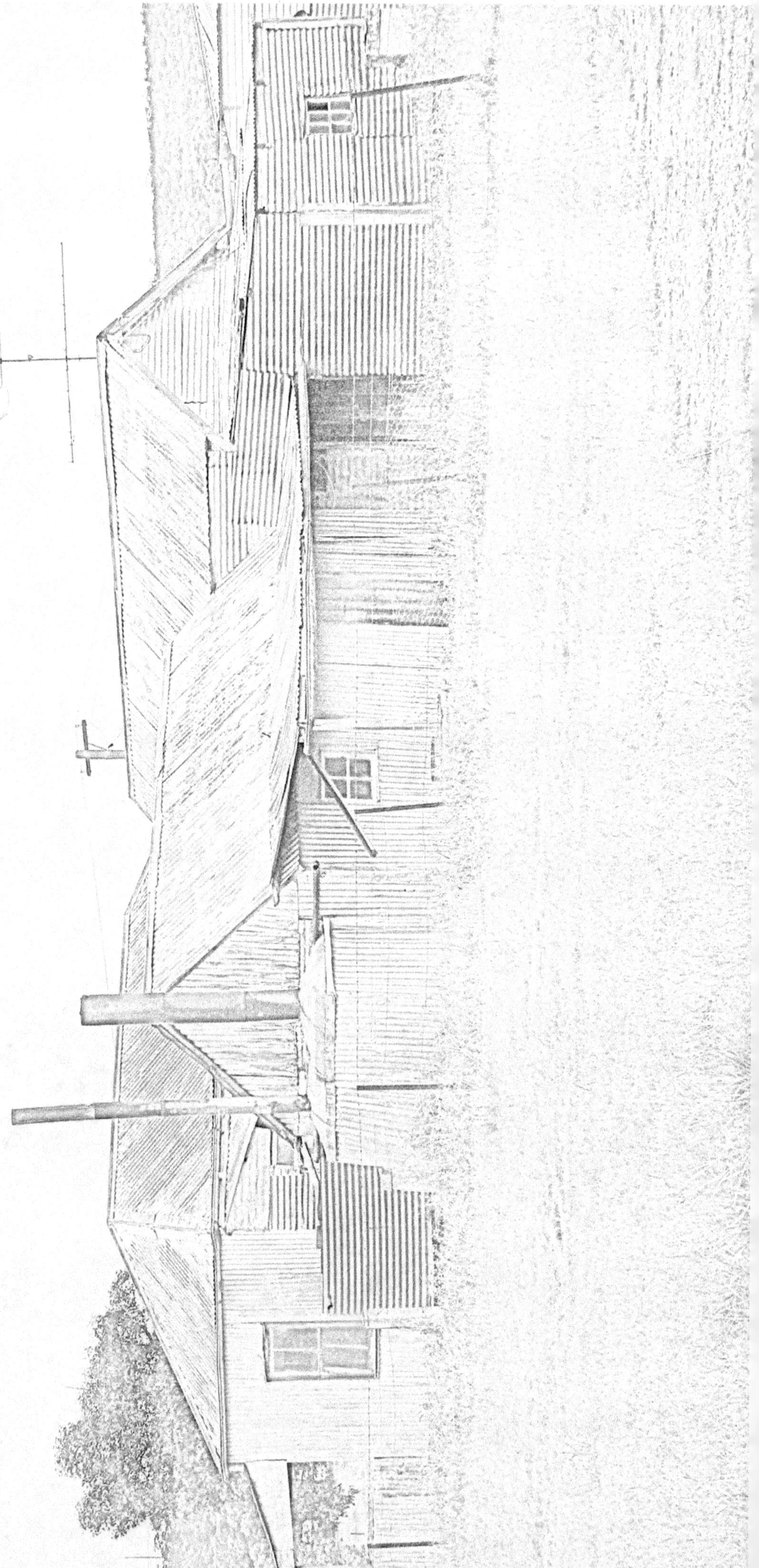

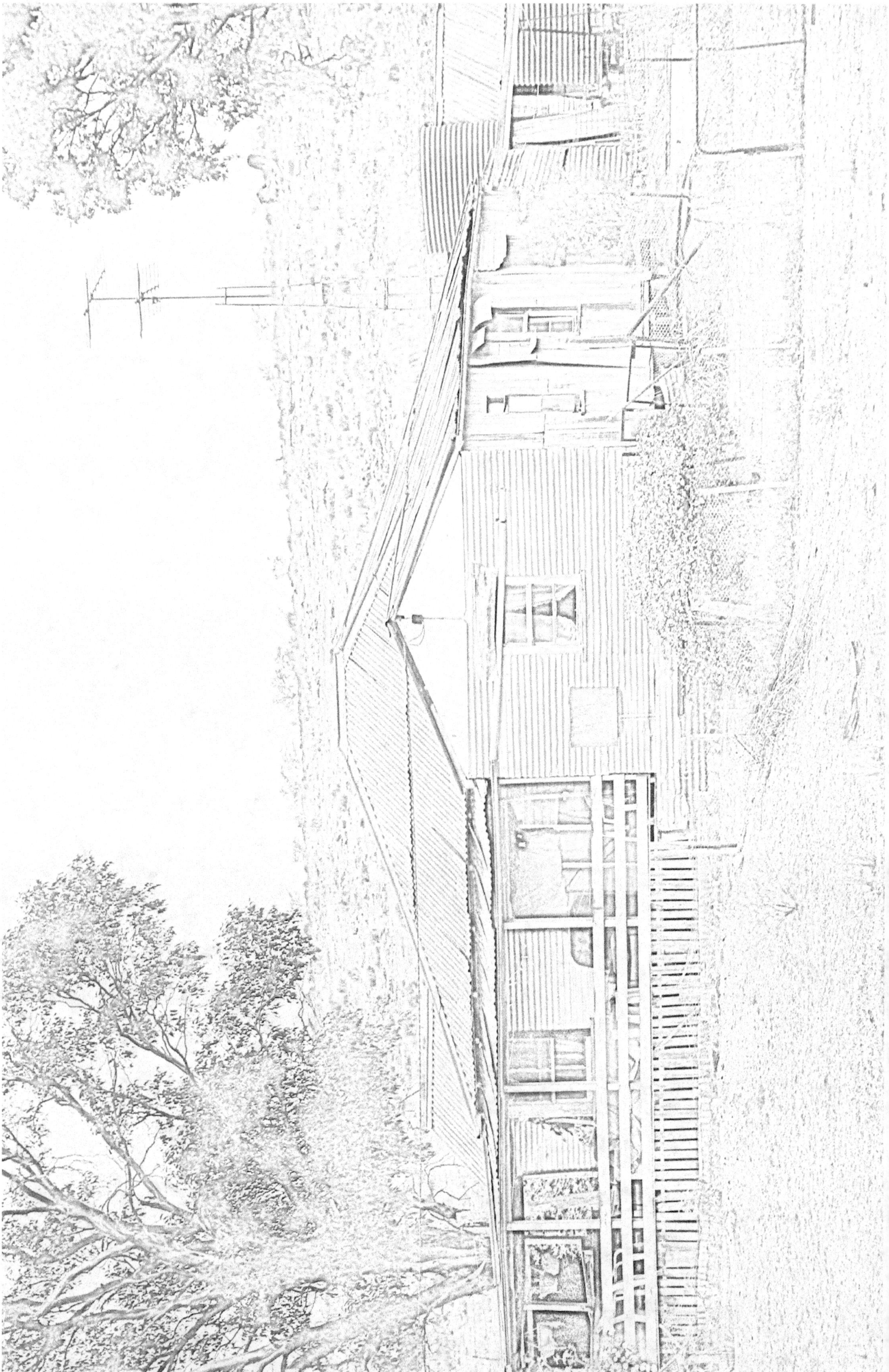

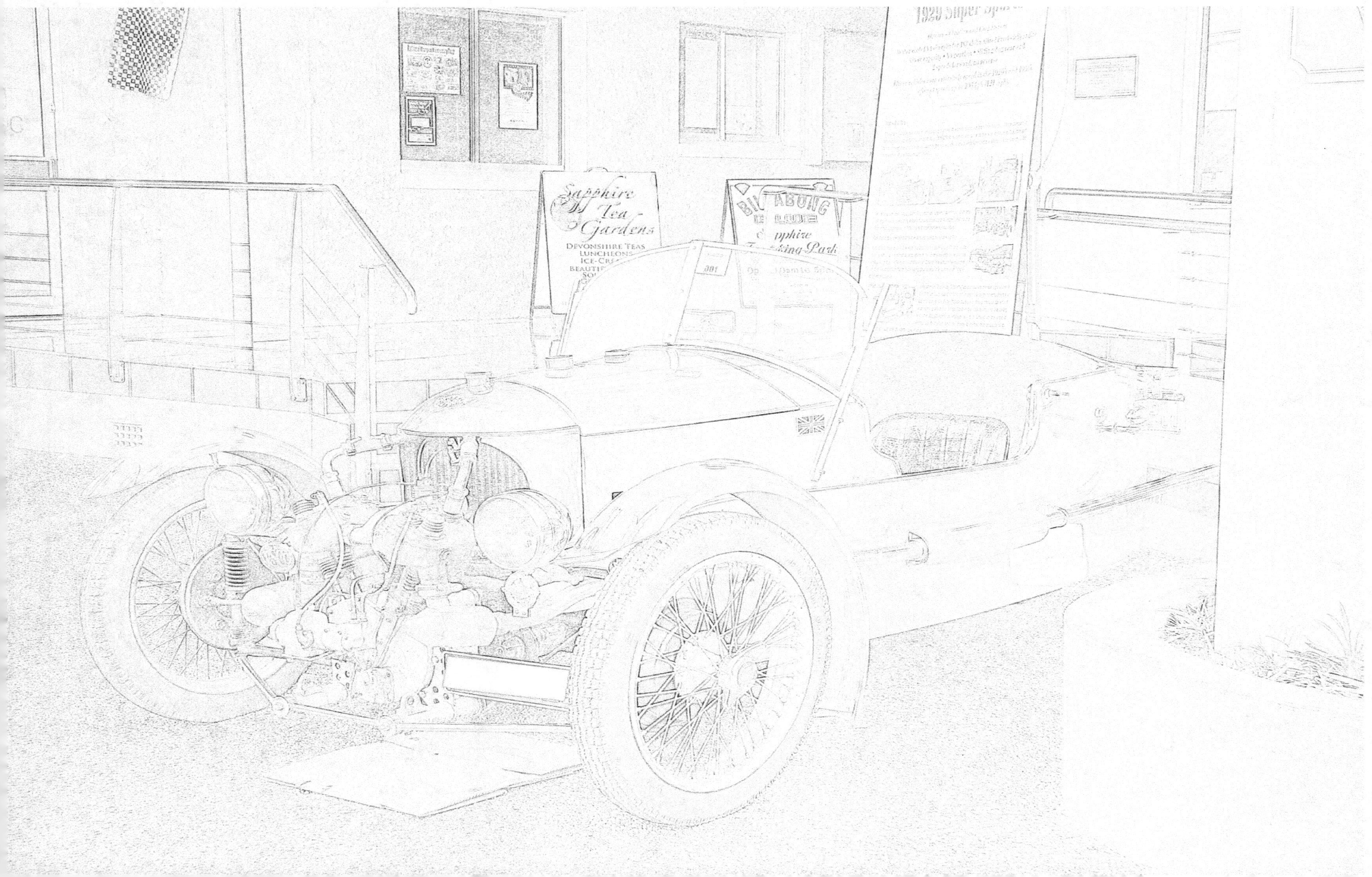

Sapphire Tea Gardens
DEVONSHIRE TEAS
LUNCHEONS

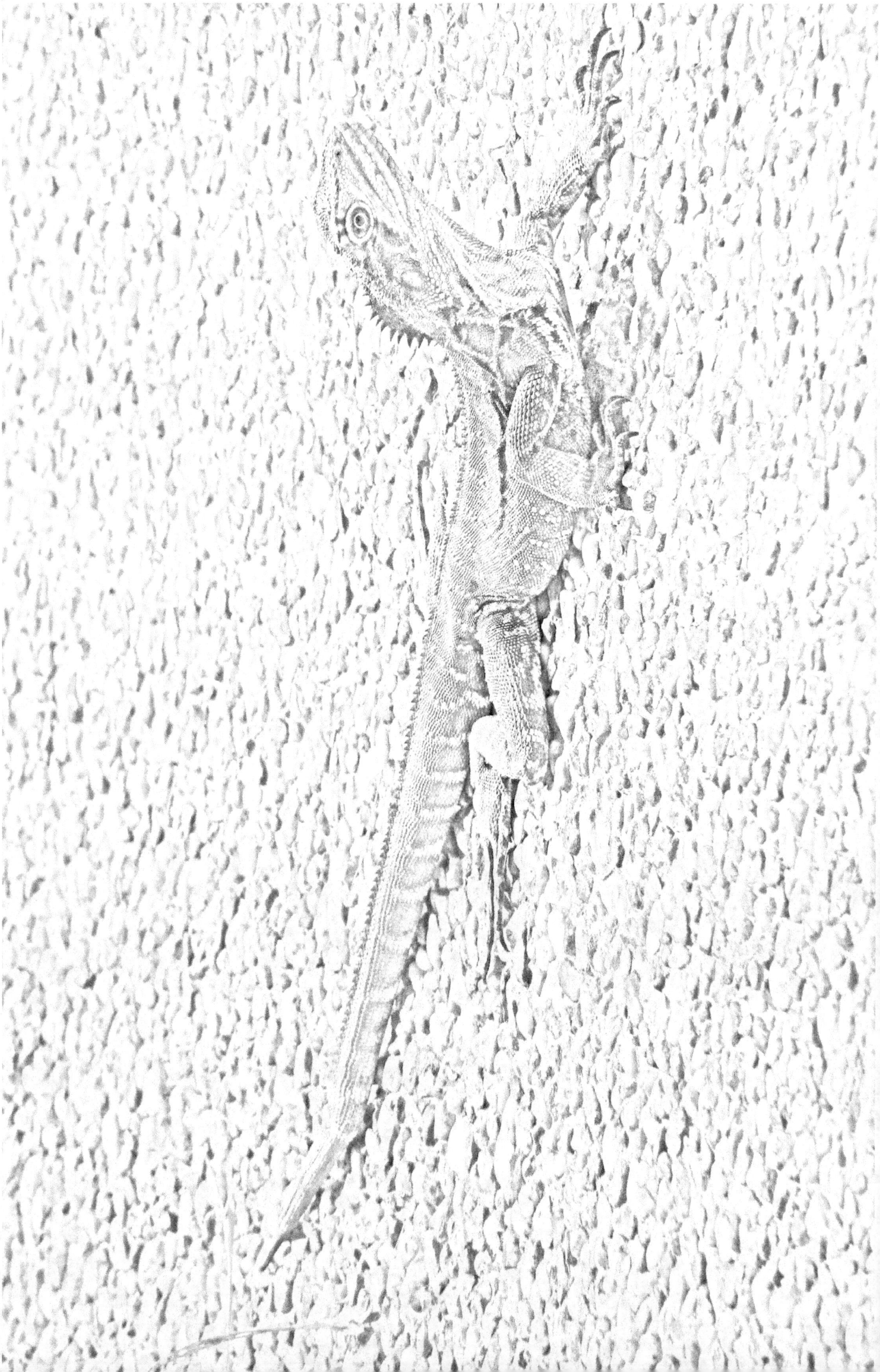

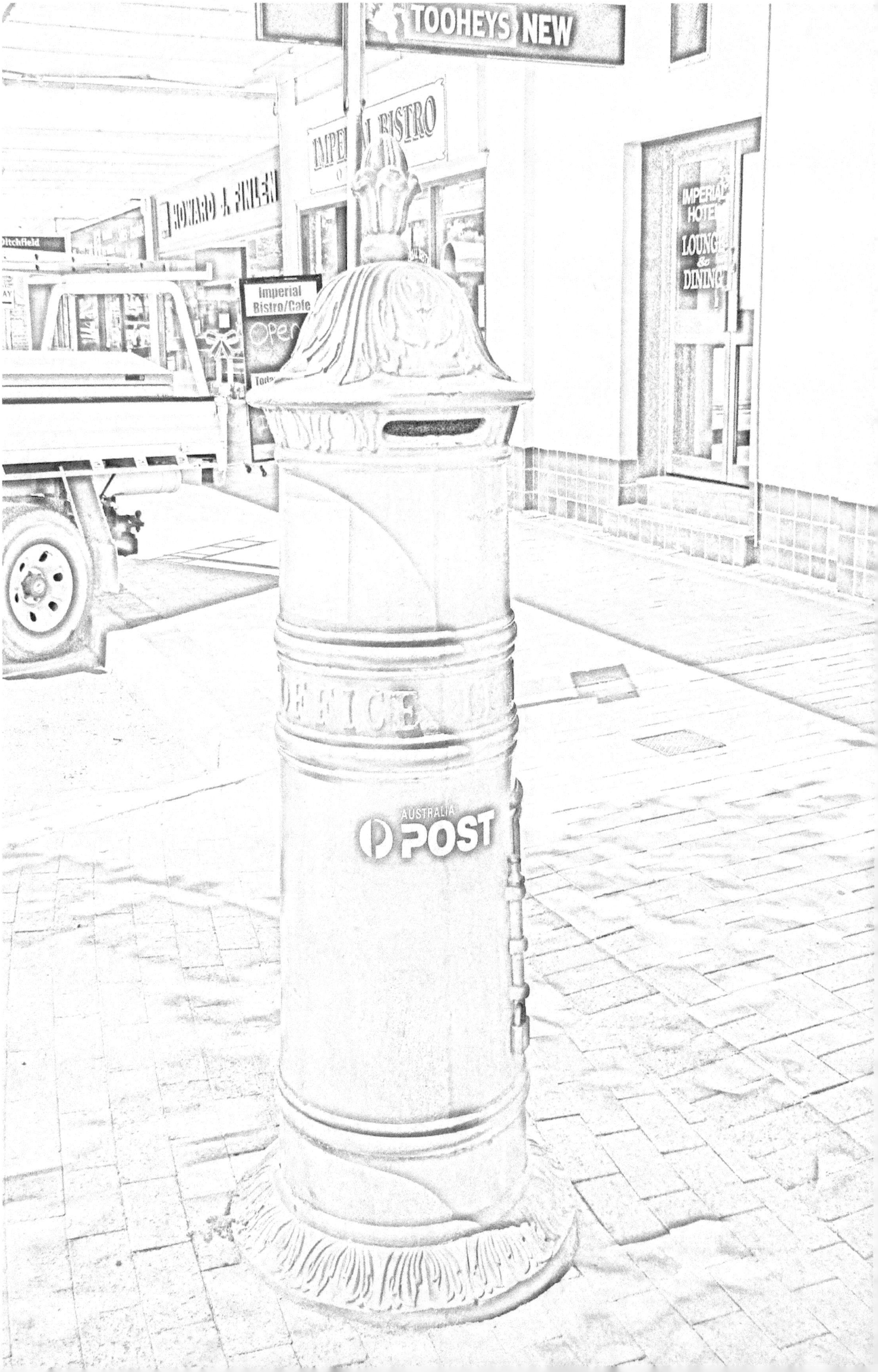
TOOHEYS NEW
HOWARD J. FINLEN
Imperial
Bistro/Cafe
Open
AUSTRALIA
POST

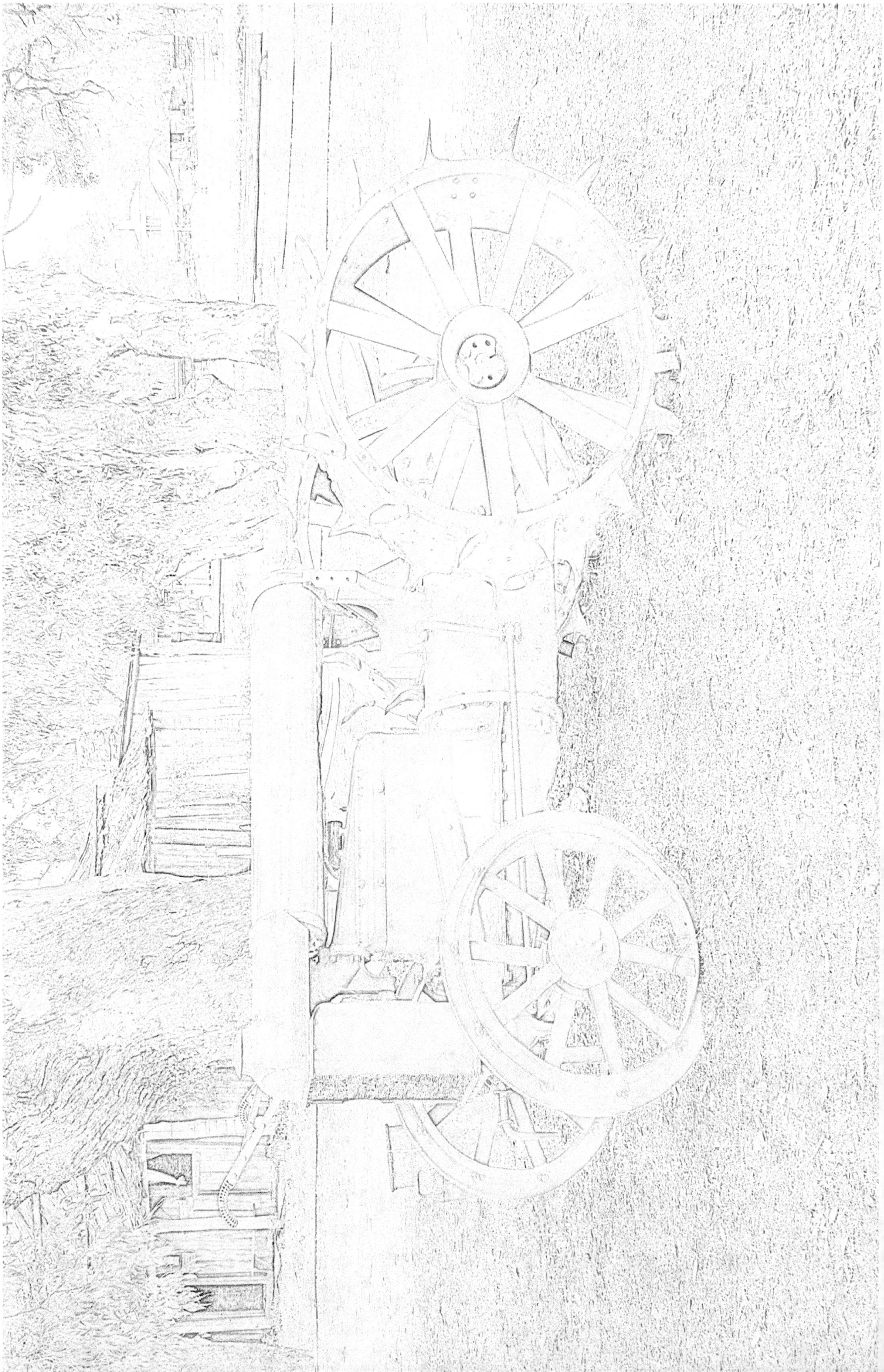

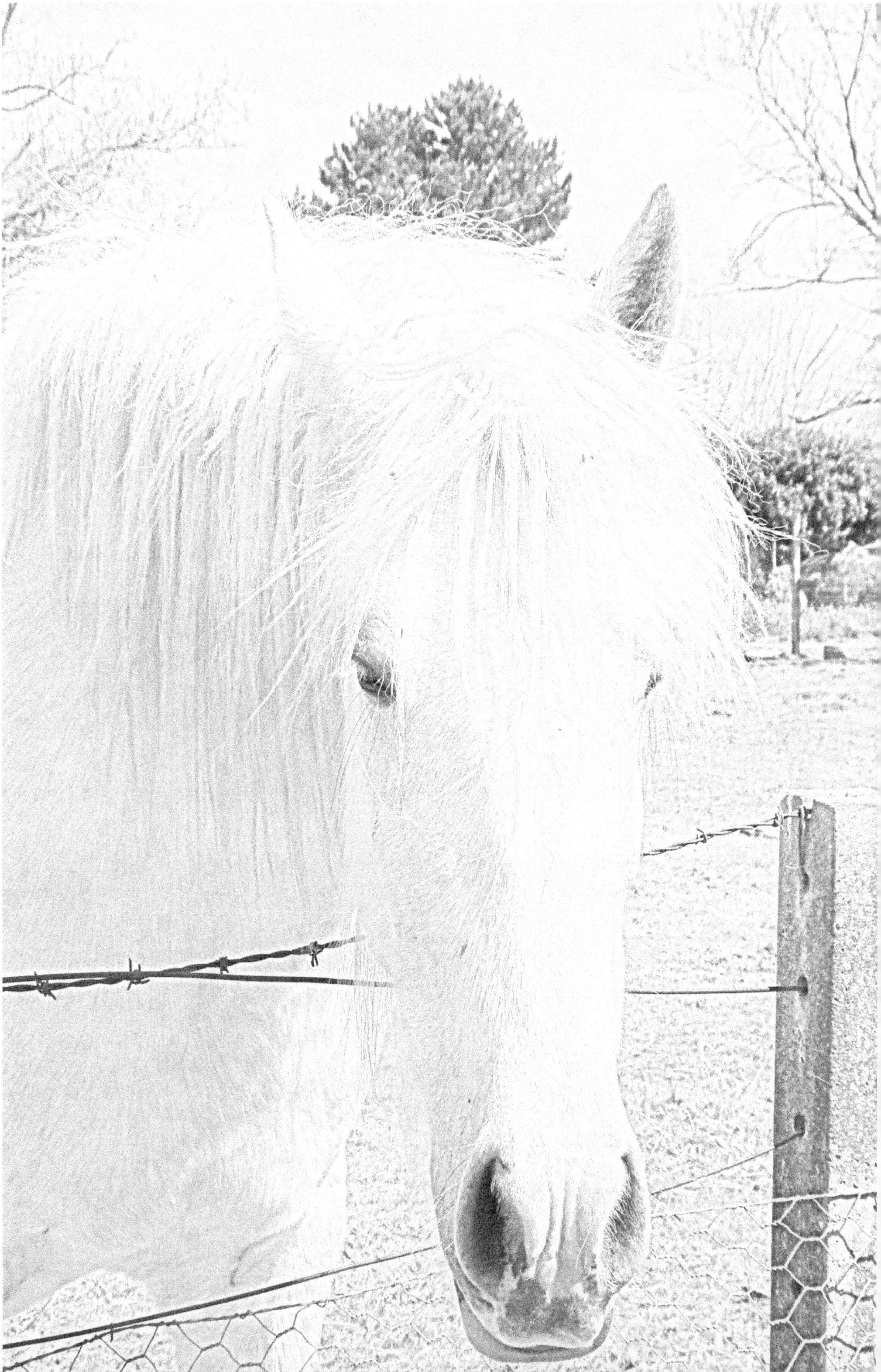

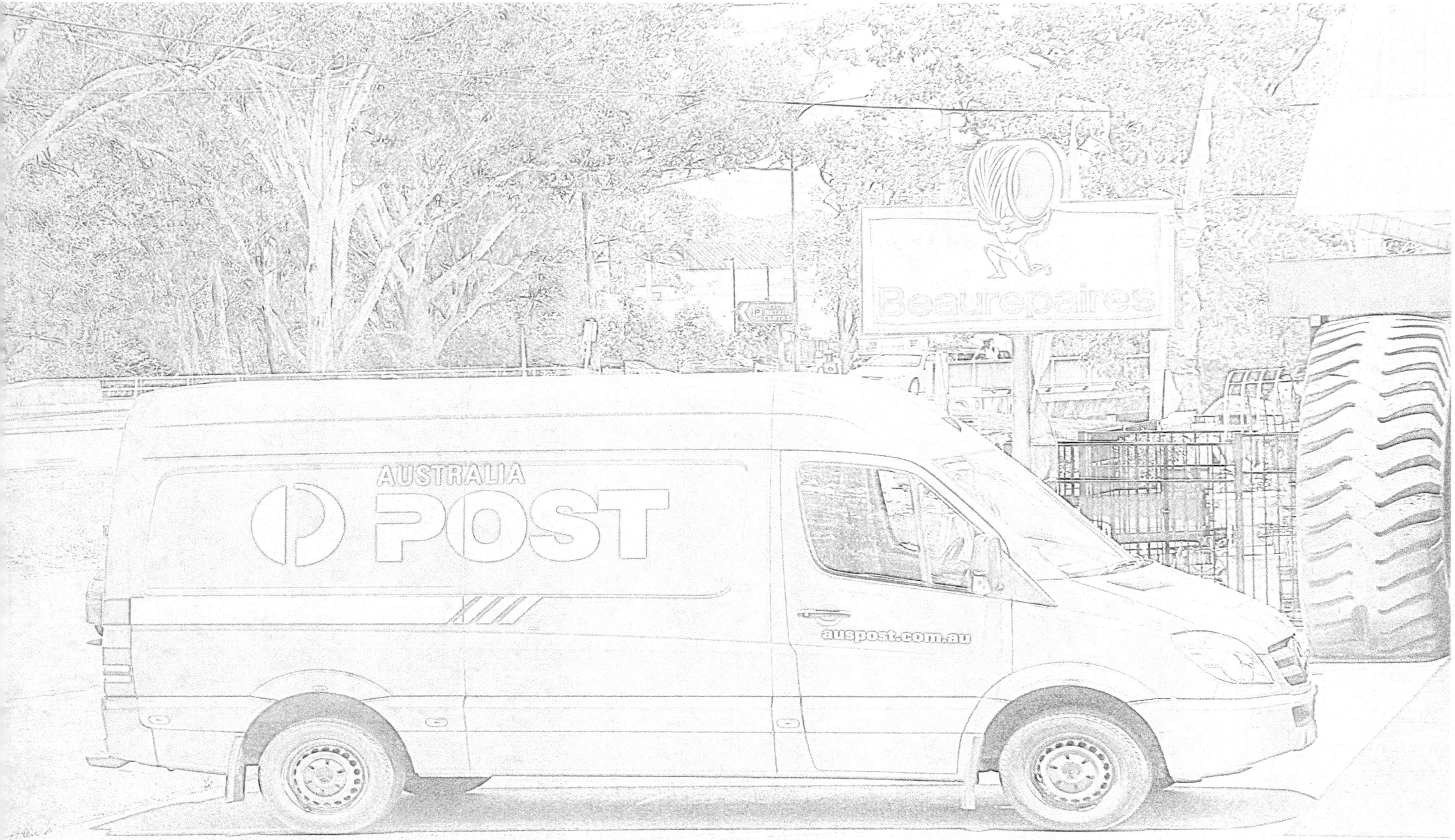
Beaurepaires
AUSTRALIA
POST
auspost.com.au

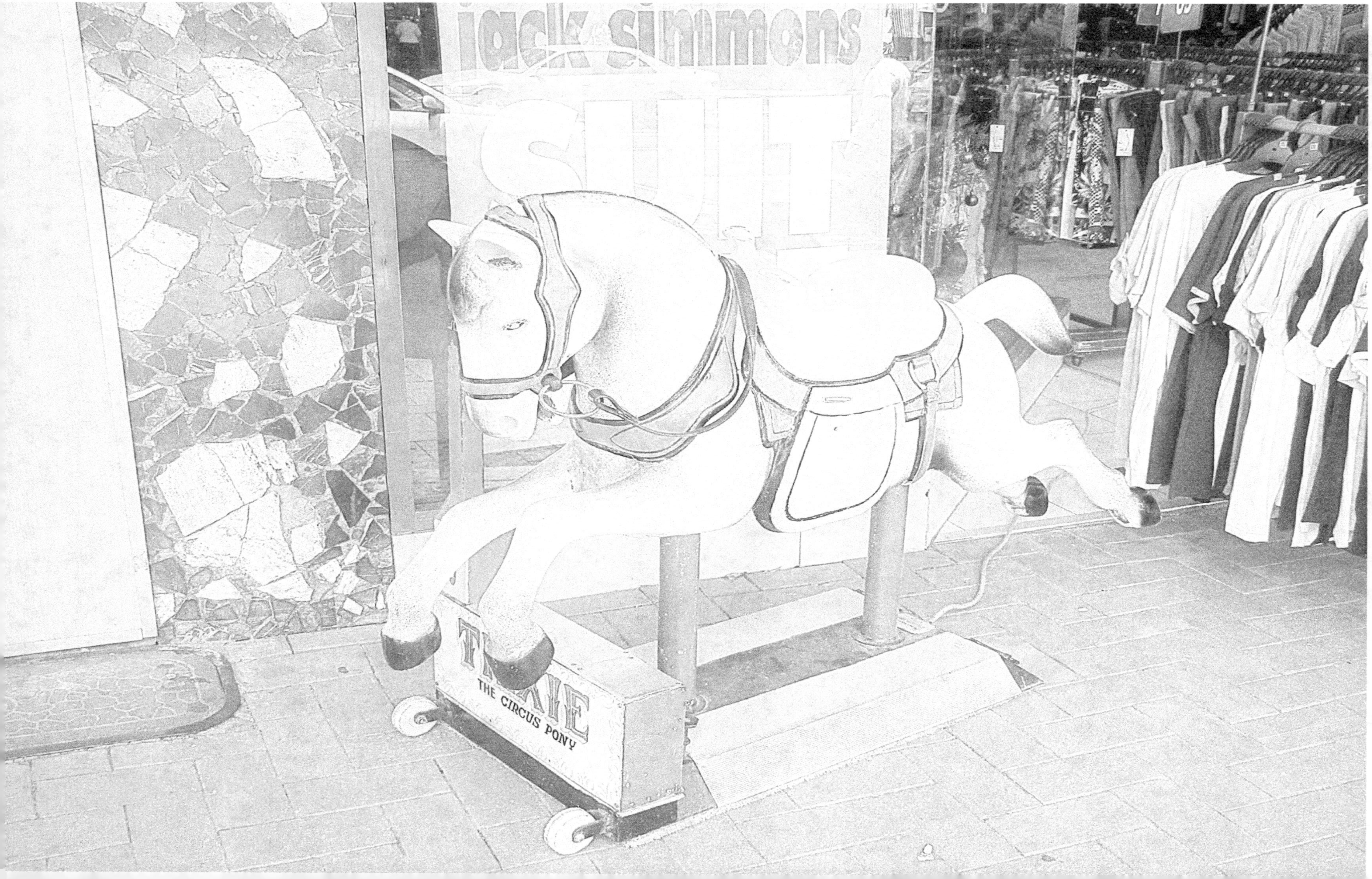
jack simmons
TRIXIE
THE CIRCUS PONY

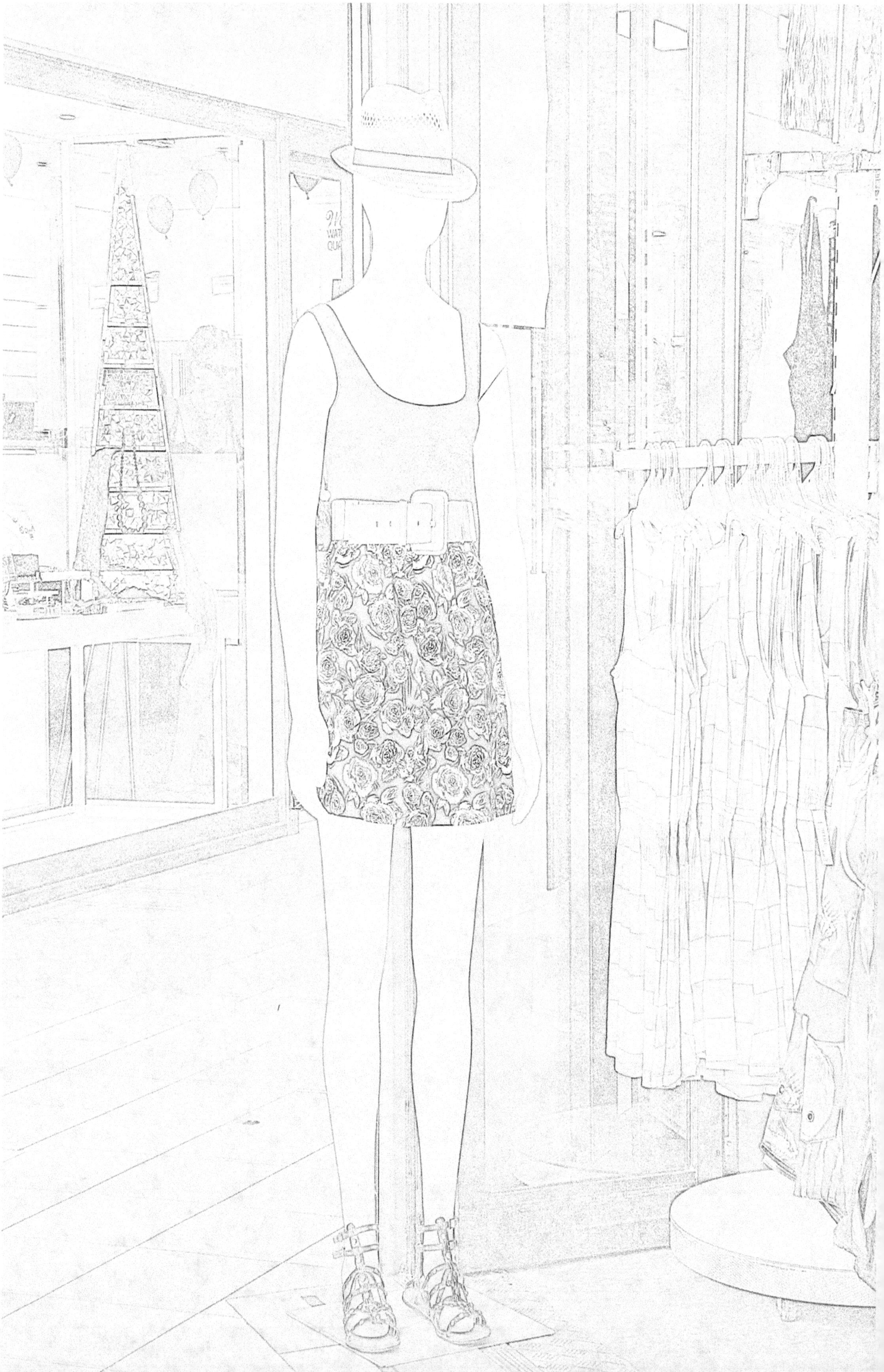

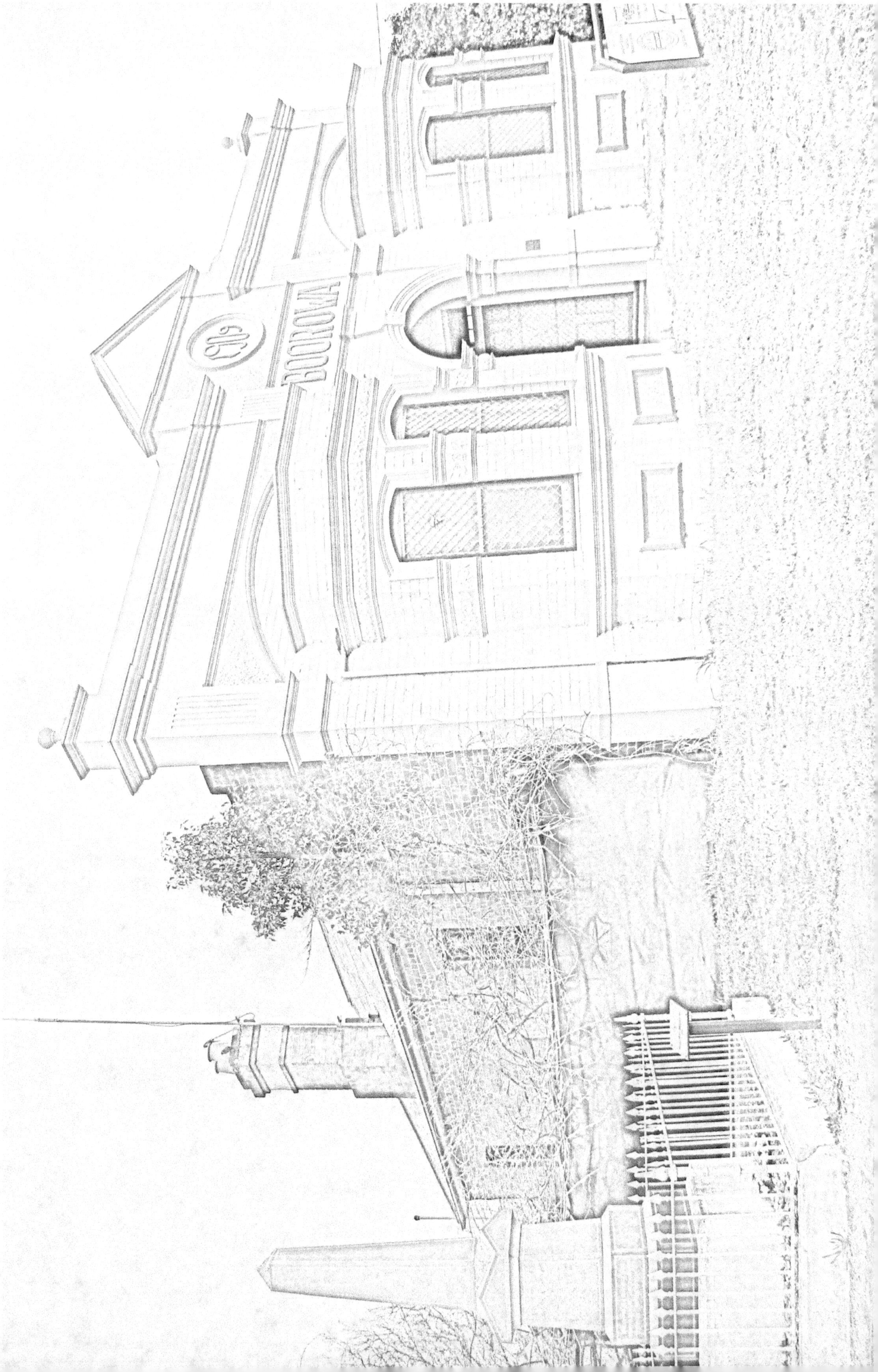
BOOROWA

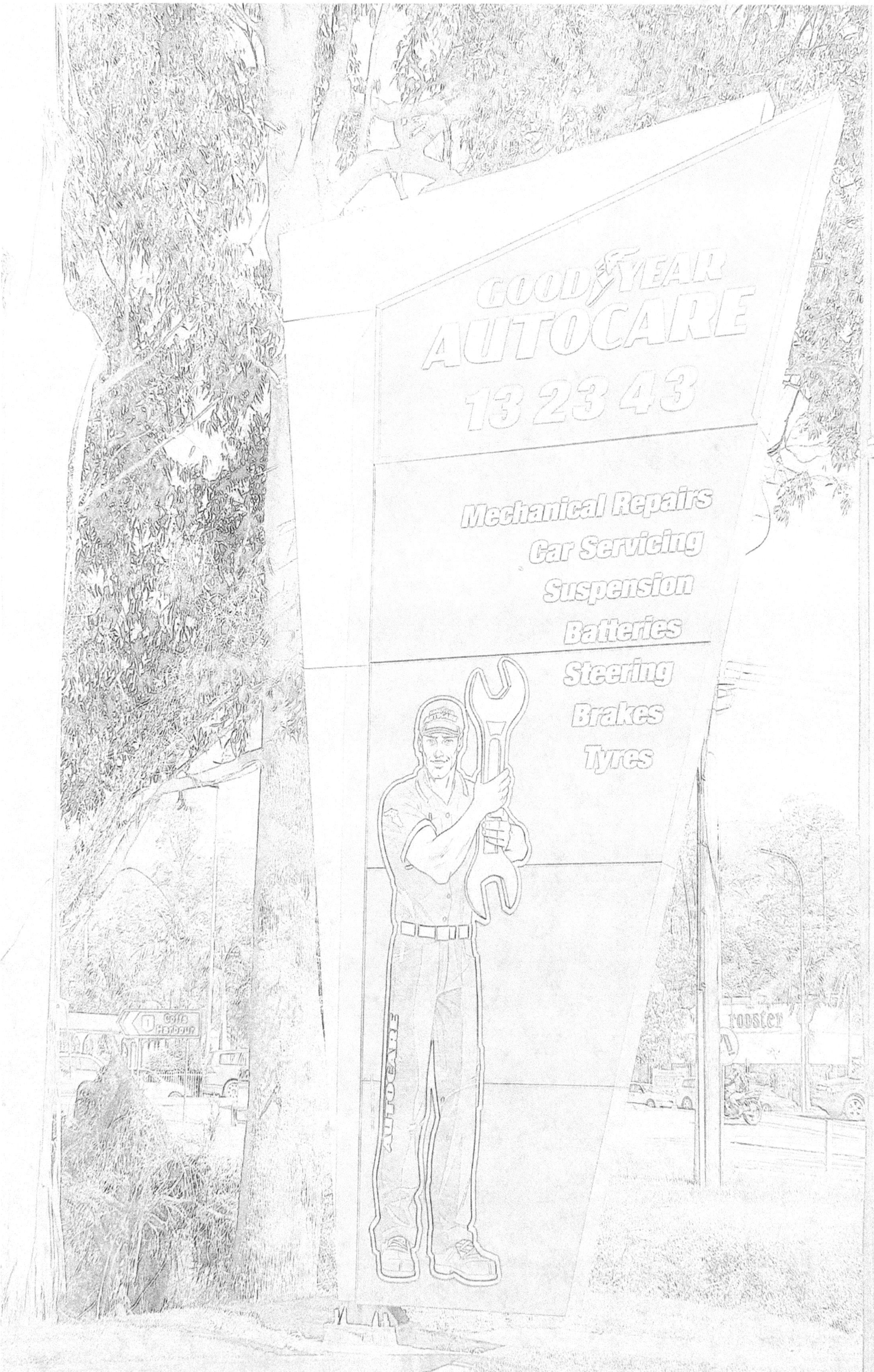
GOODYEAR
AUTOCARE
13 23 43
Mechanical Repairs
Car Servicing
Suspension
Batteries
Steering
Brakes
Tyres
AUTOCARE
rooster

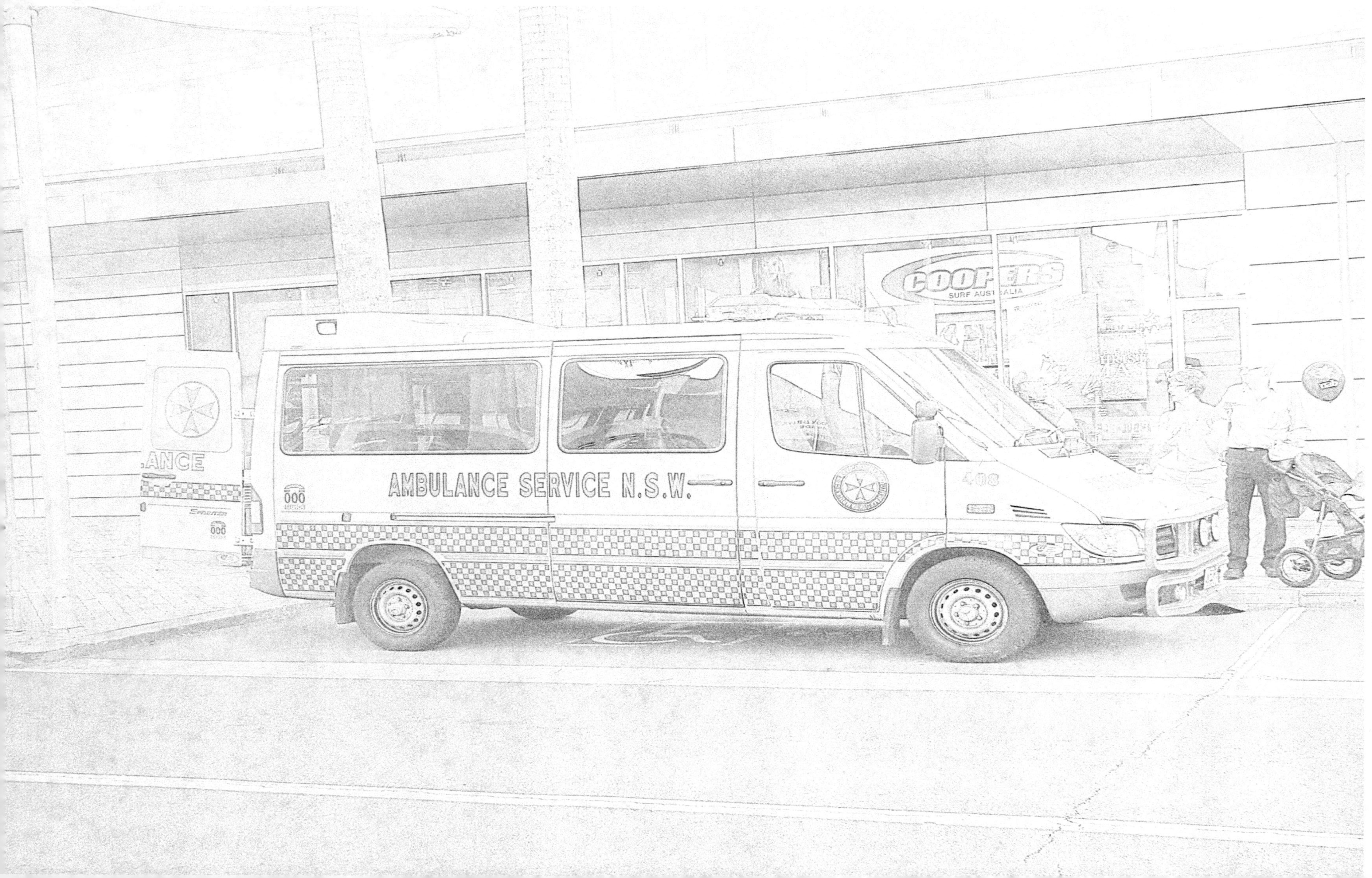
COOPERS
SURF AUSTRALIA
AMBULANCE SERVICE N.S.W.
408
000
ANCE
000

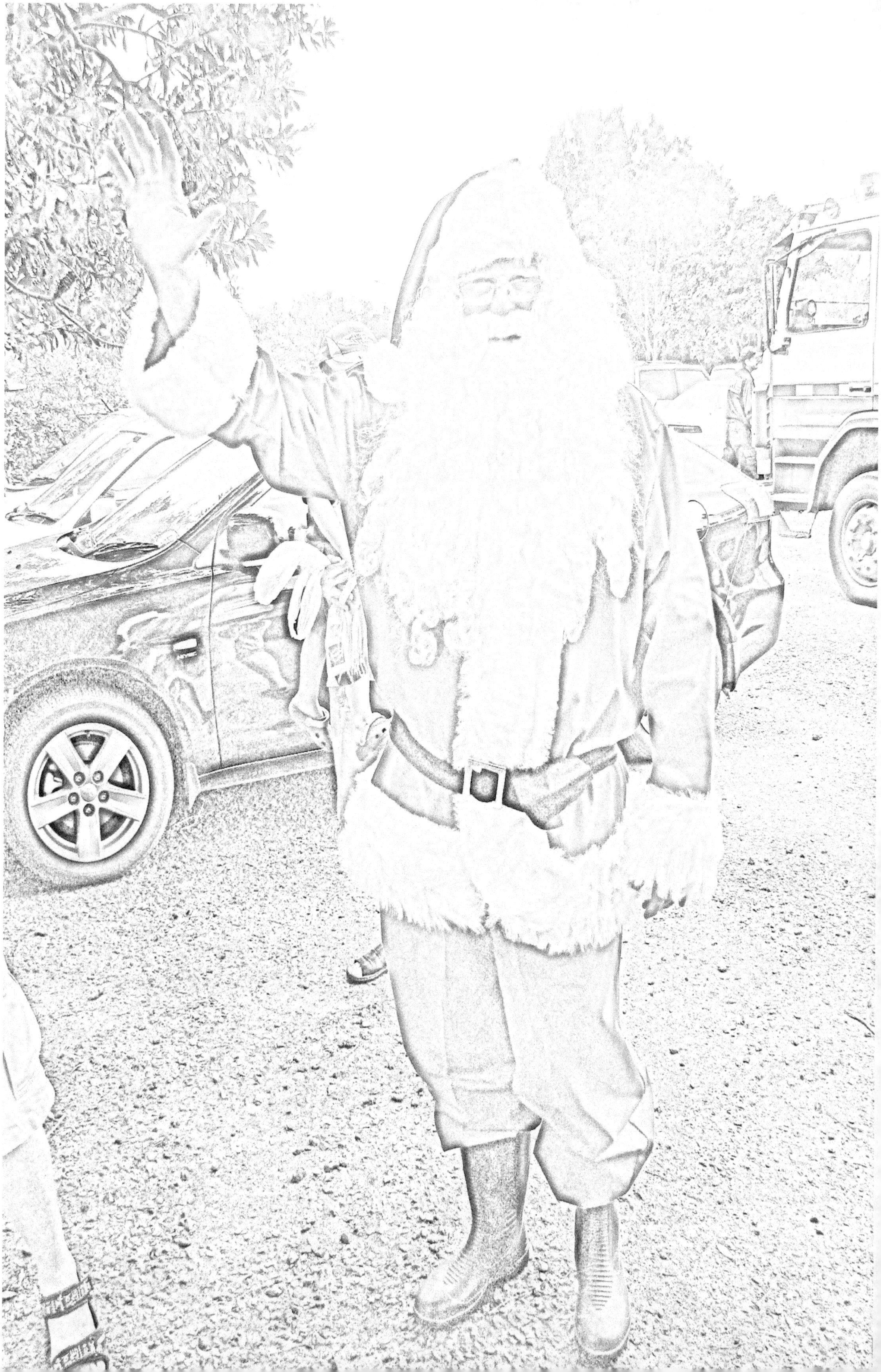

Coca-Cola
AUSTRALIA CAFE
DINE IN — TAKE AWAY
AUSTRALIA CAFE
FOR LEASE

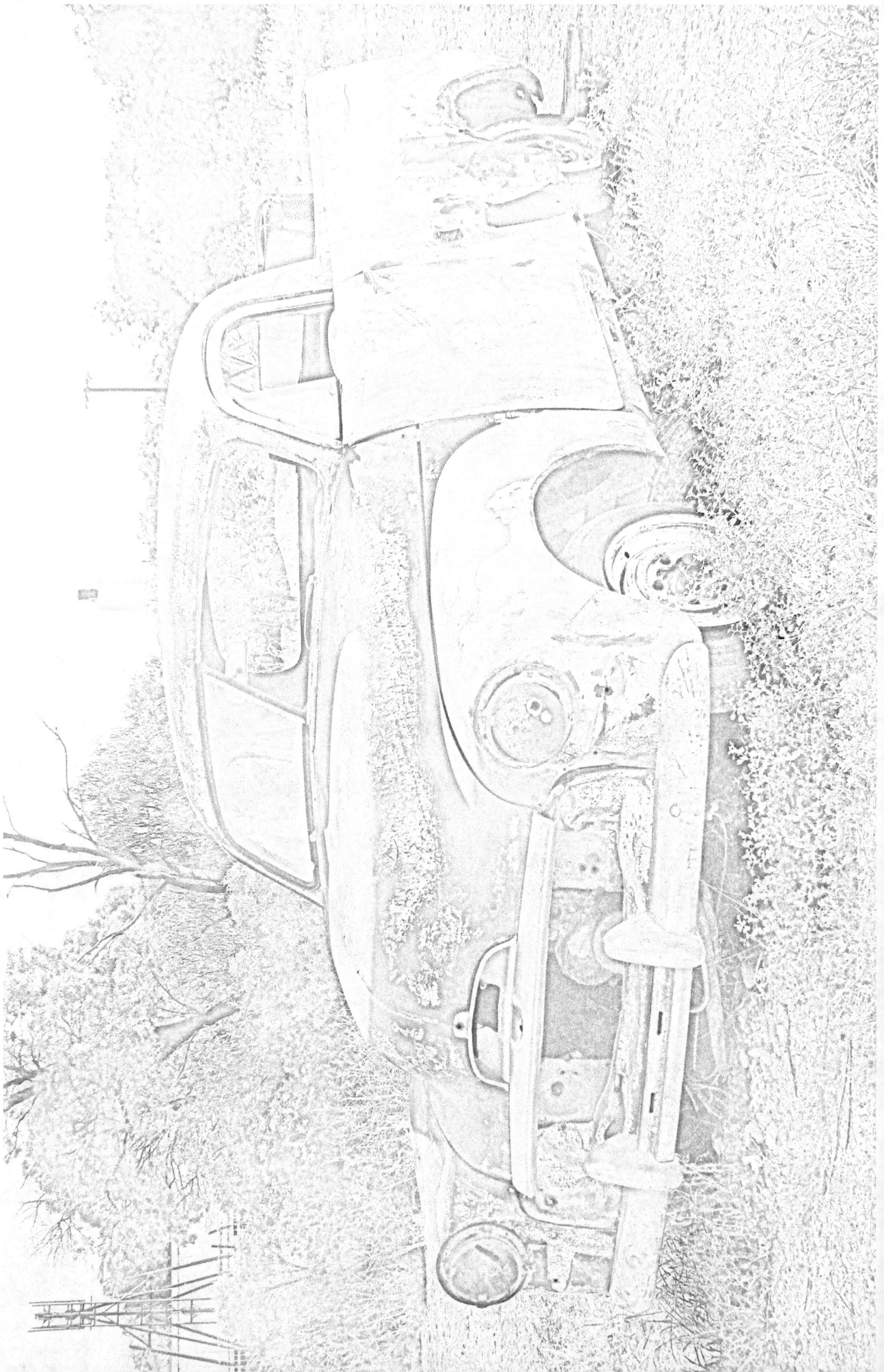

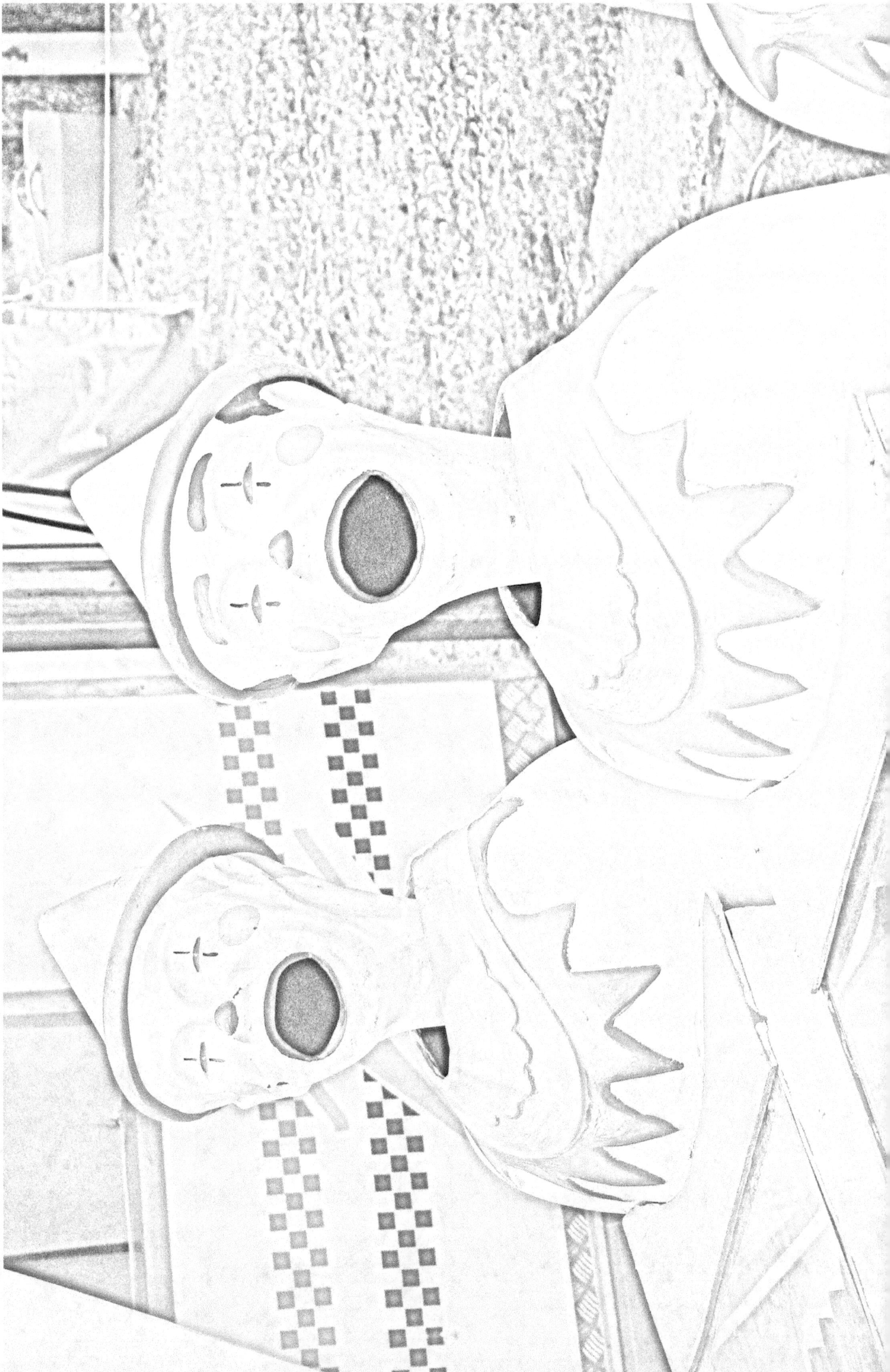

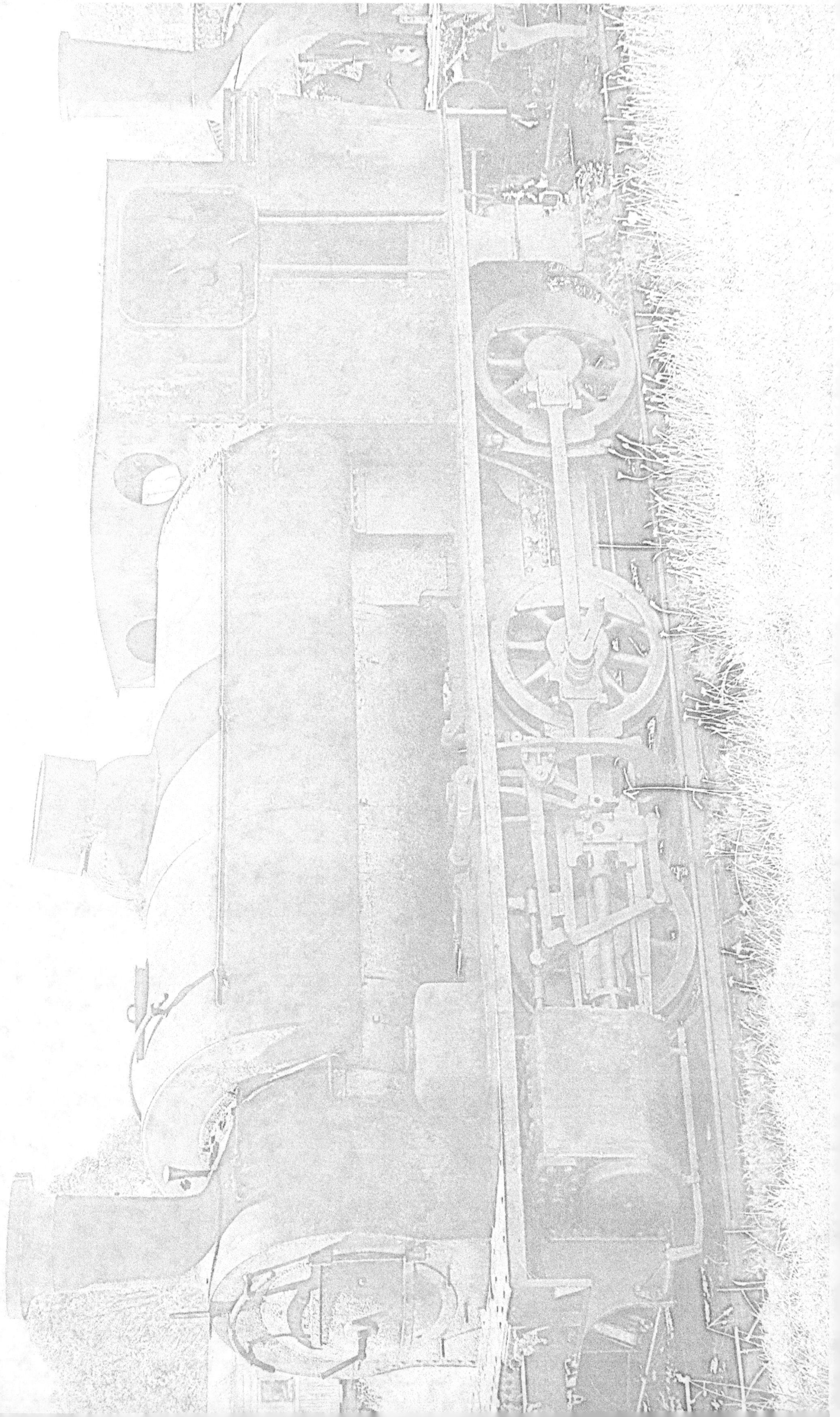

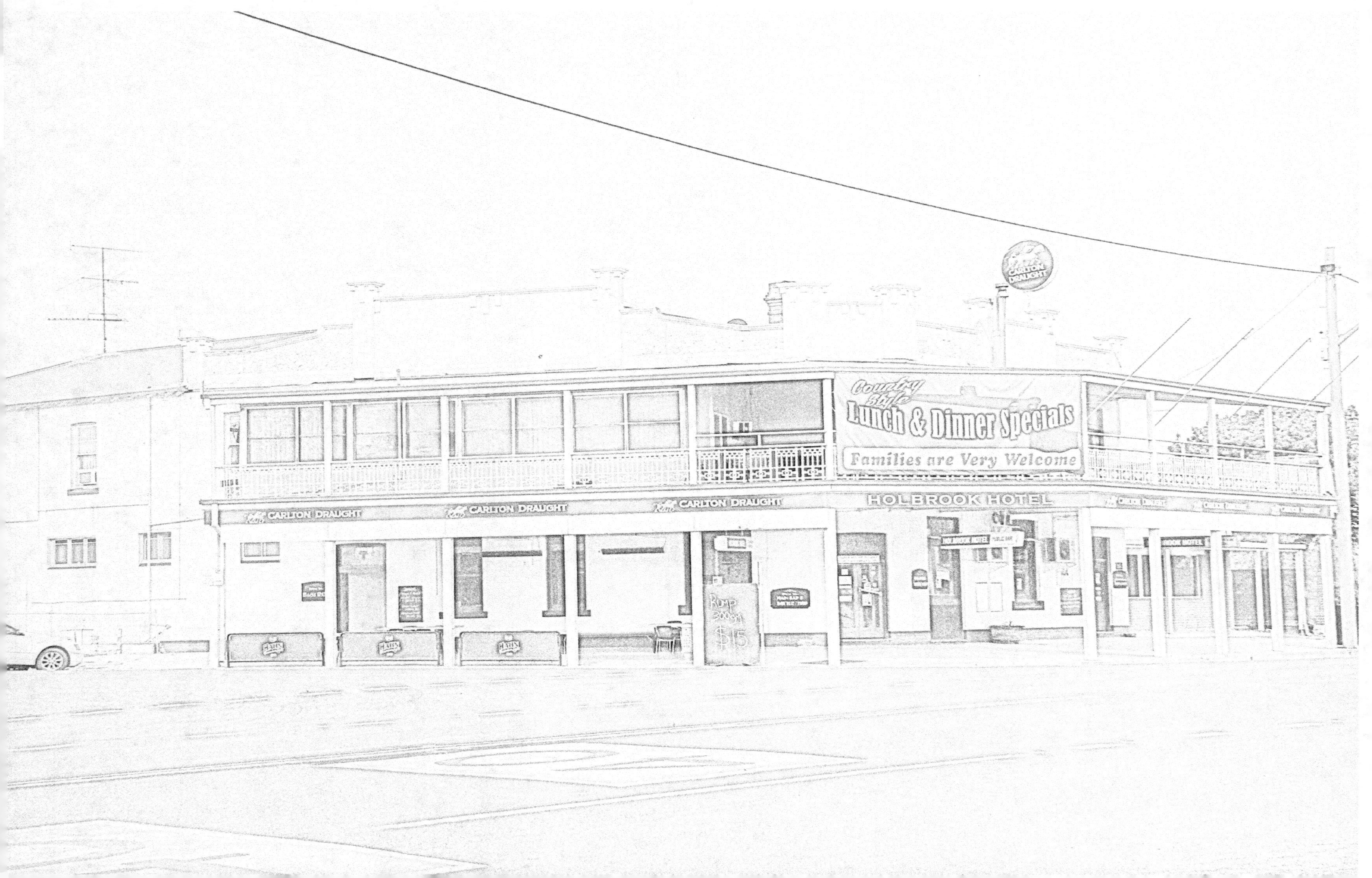
Country Style
Lunch & Dinner Specials
Families are Very Welcome
HOLBROOK HOTEL
CARLTON DRAUGHT
CARLTON DRAUGHT
CARLTON DRAUGHT
Rump 300gm $15

LFB 1057/0

FOR LEASE

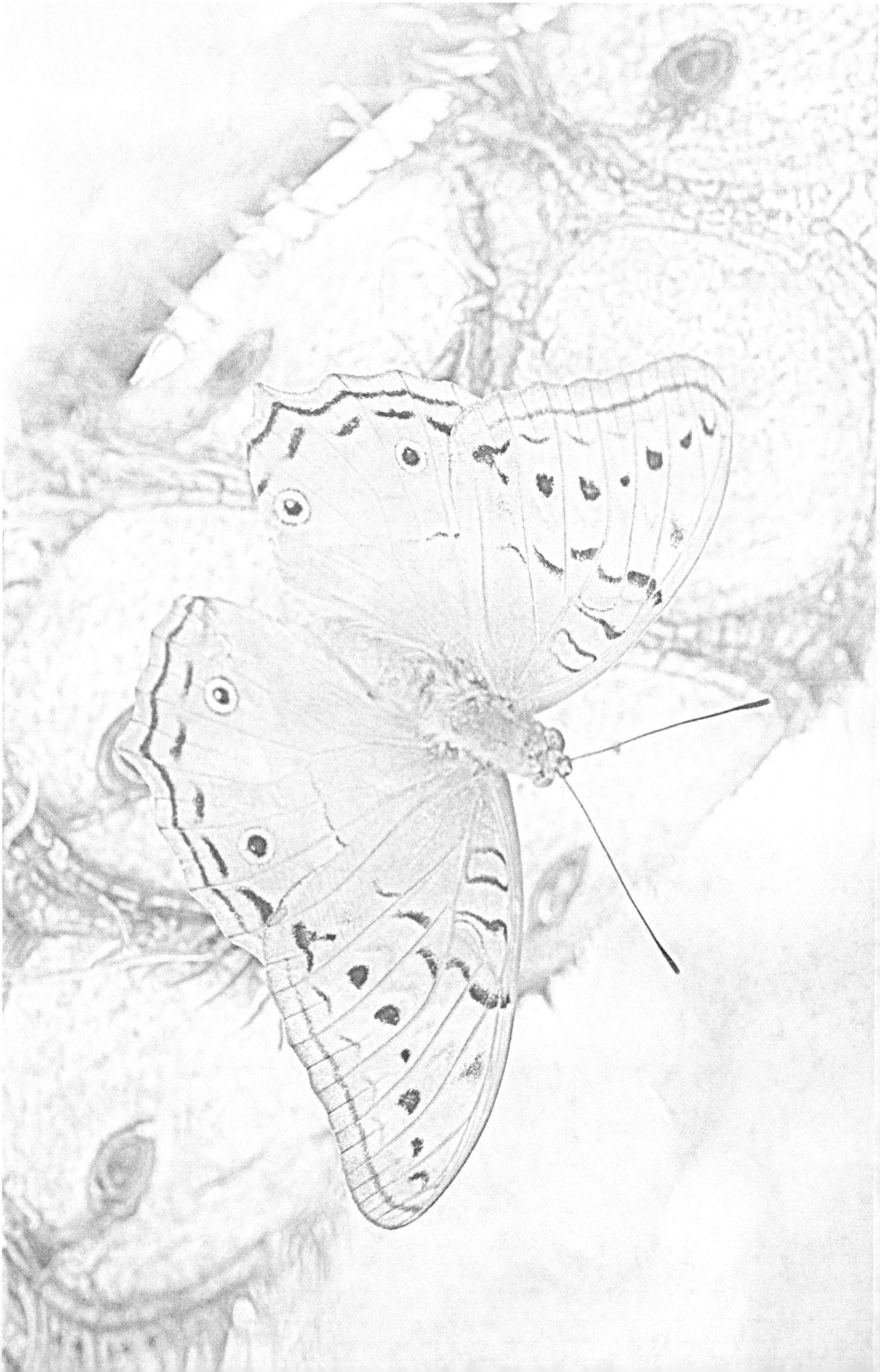

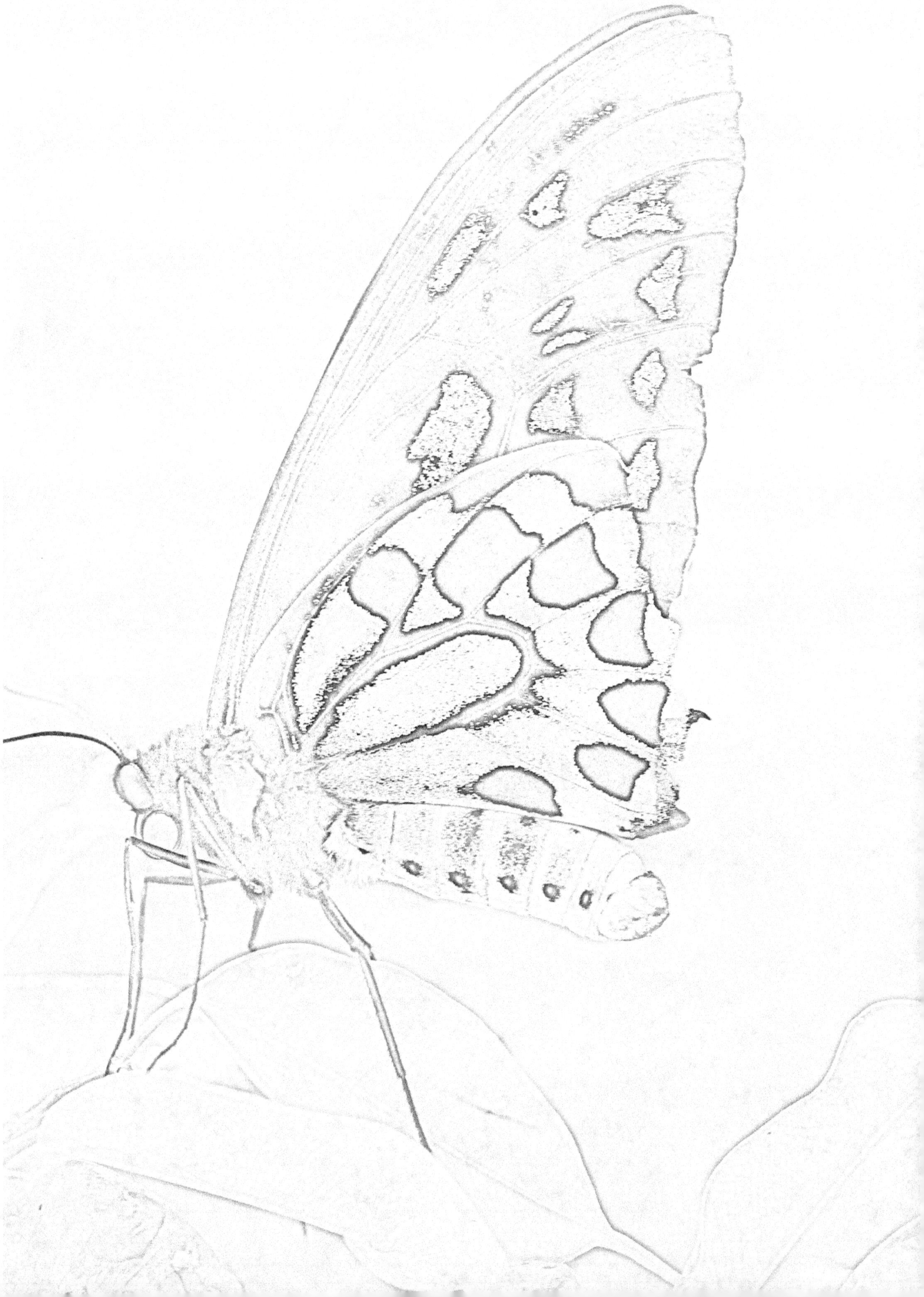

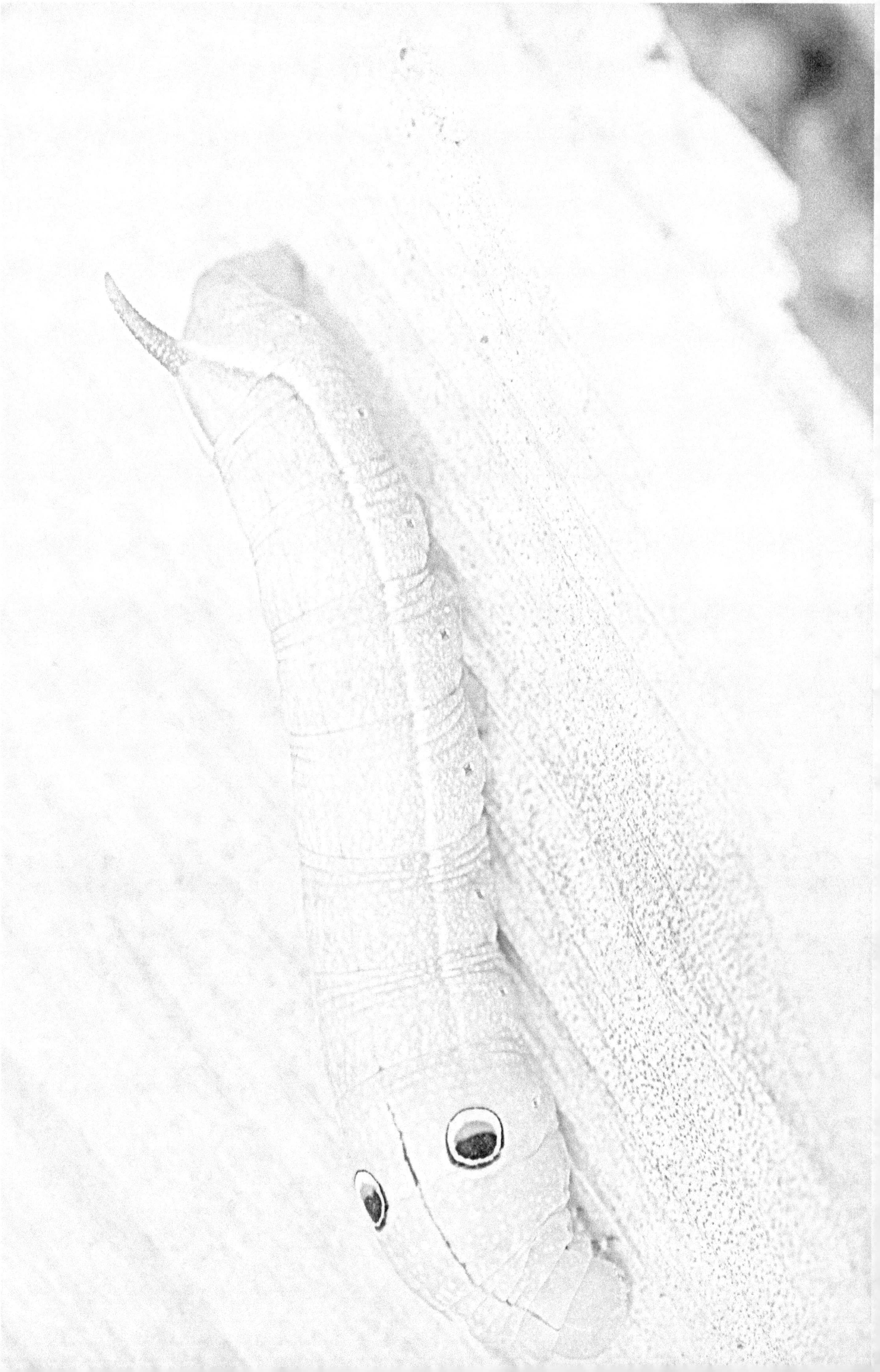

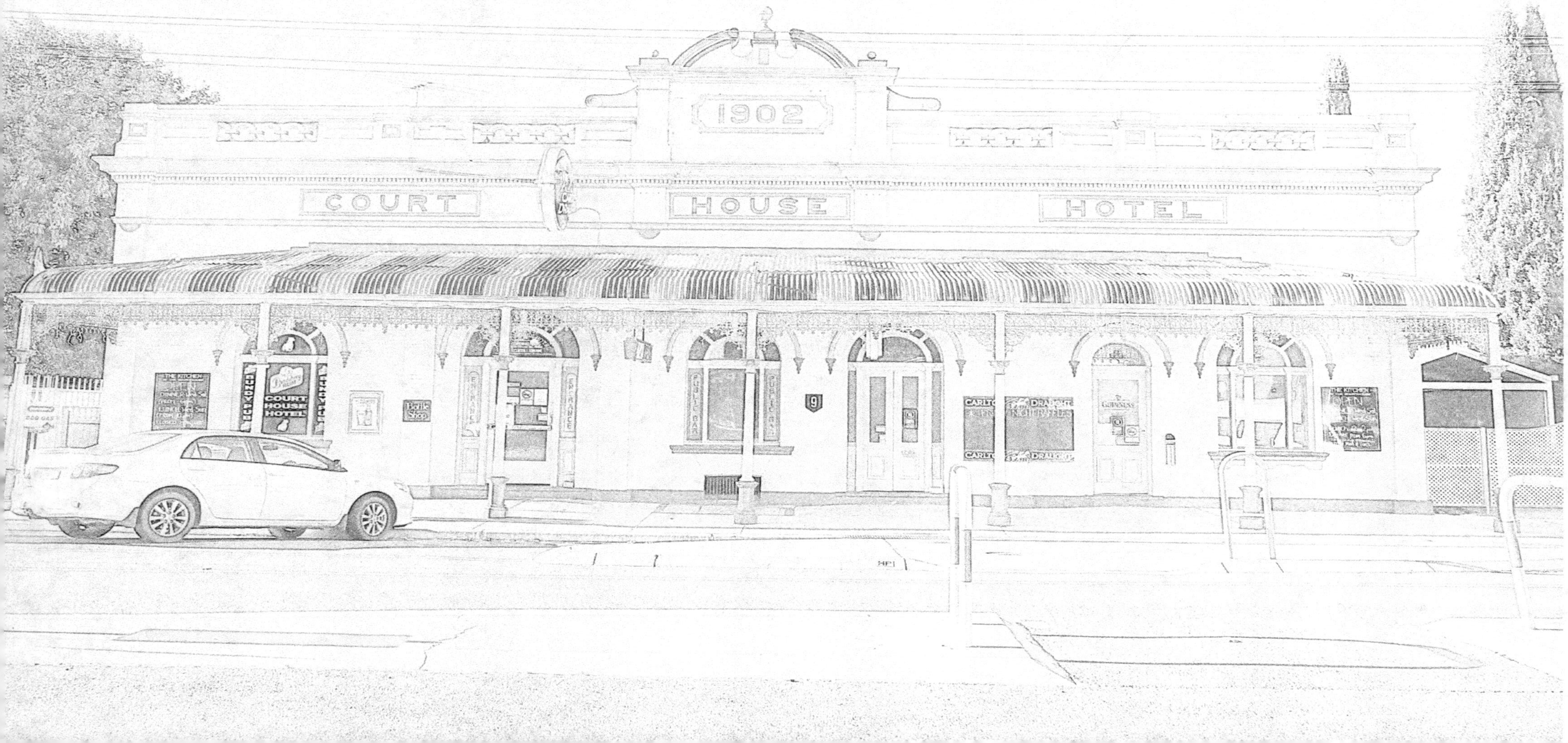
1902
COURT
HOUSE
HOTEL
COURT HOUSE HOTEL
Bottle Shop
PUBLIC BAR
9
CARLTON DRAUGHT
GUINNESS

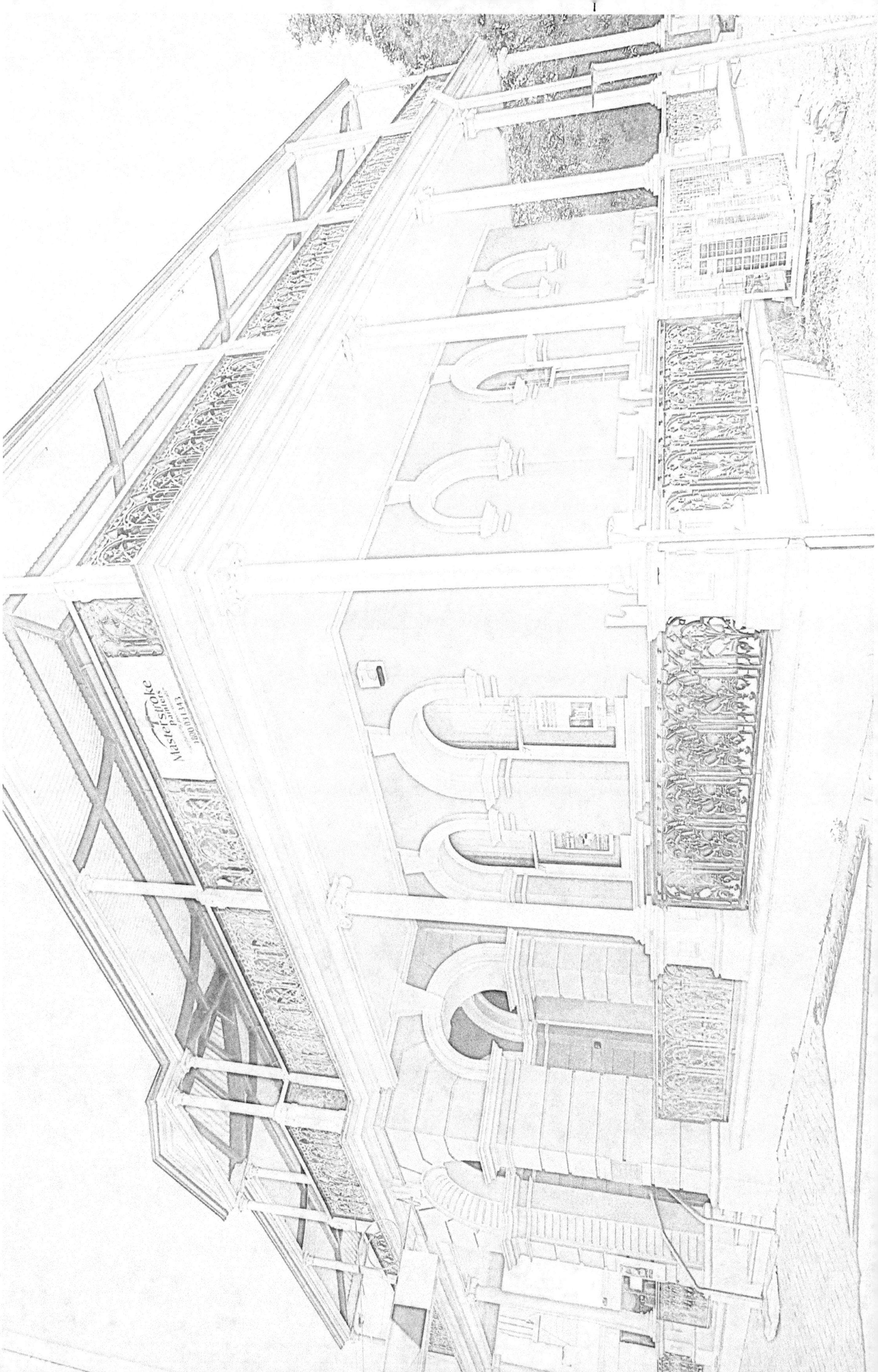
Masterstroke
painters
1800 011 343

FORBES POST OFFICE
POST
ANZAC DAY
KEEP LEFT

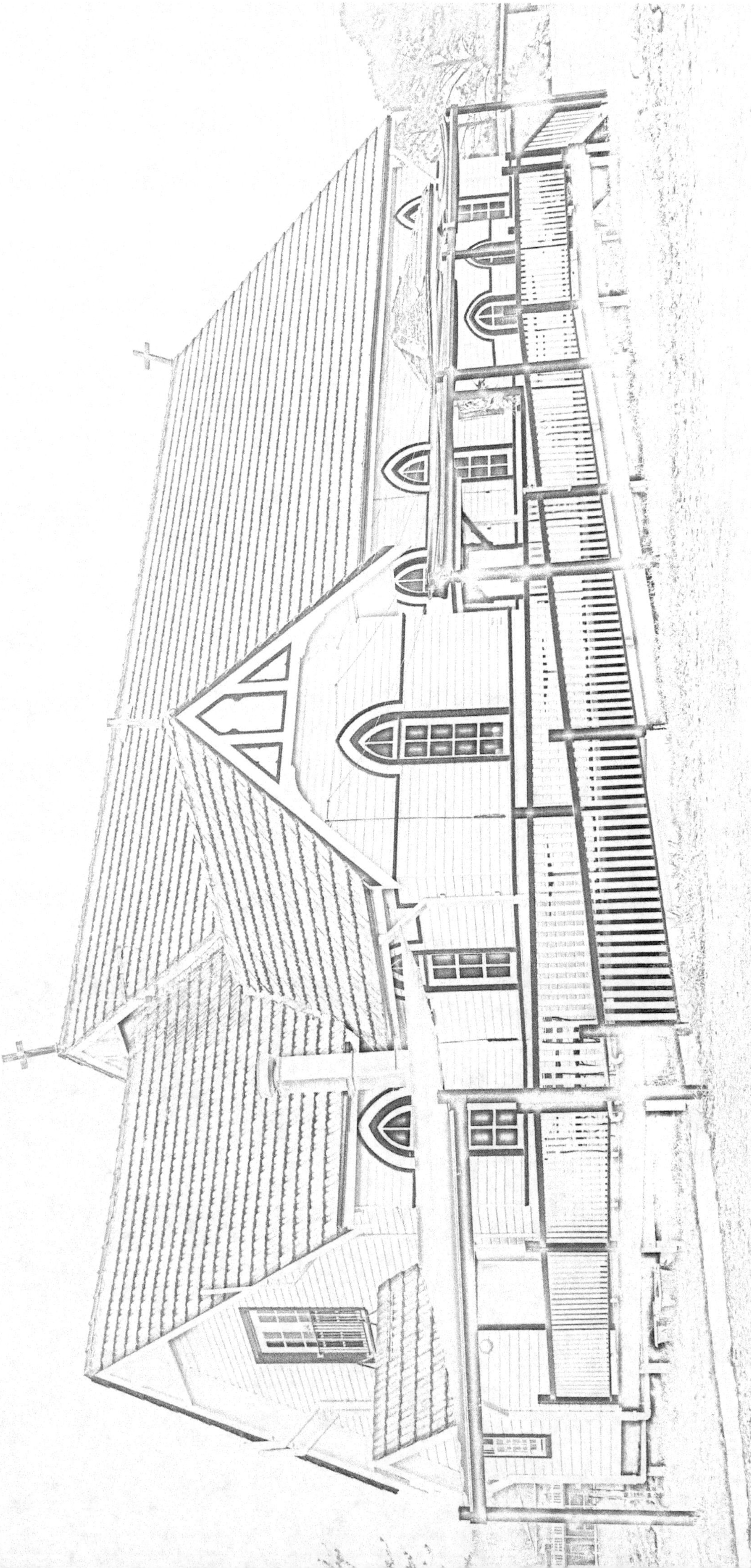

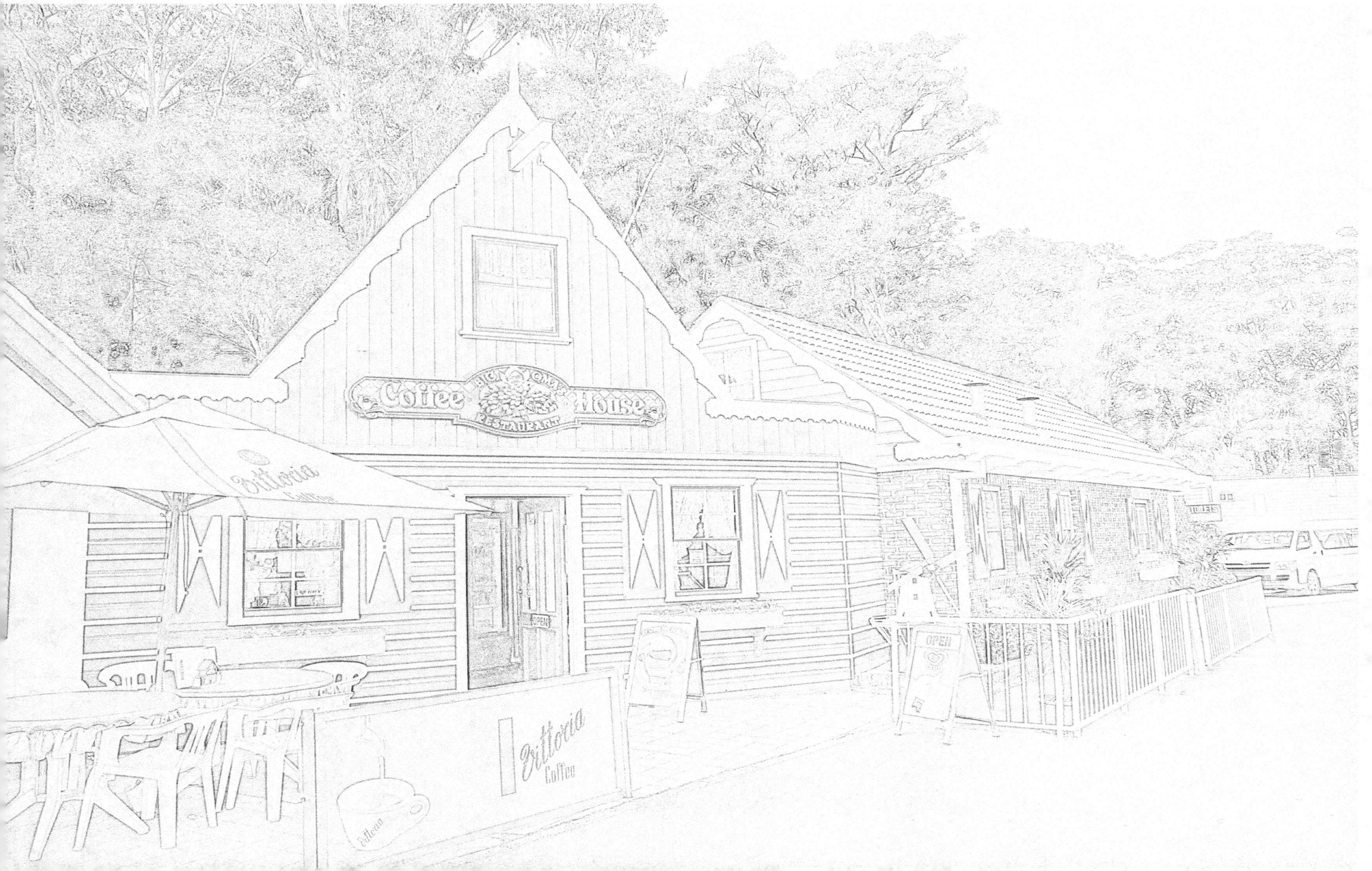
Coffee House
RESTAURANT
Vittoria
Vittoria
Coffee
OPEN
OPEN
TOILETS

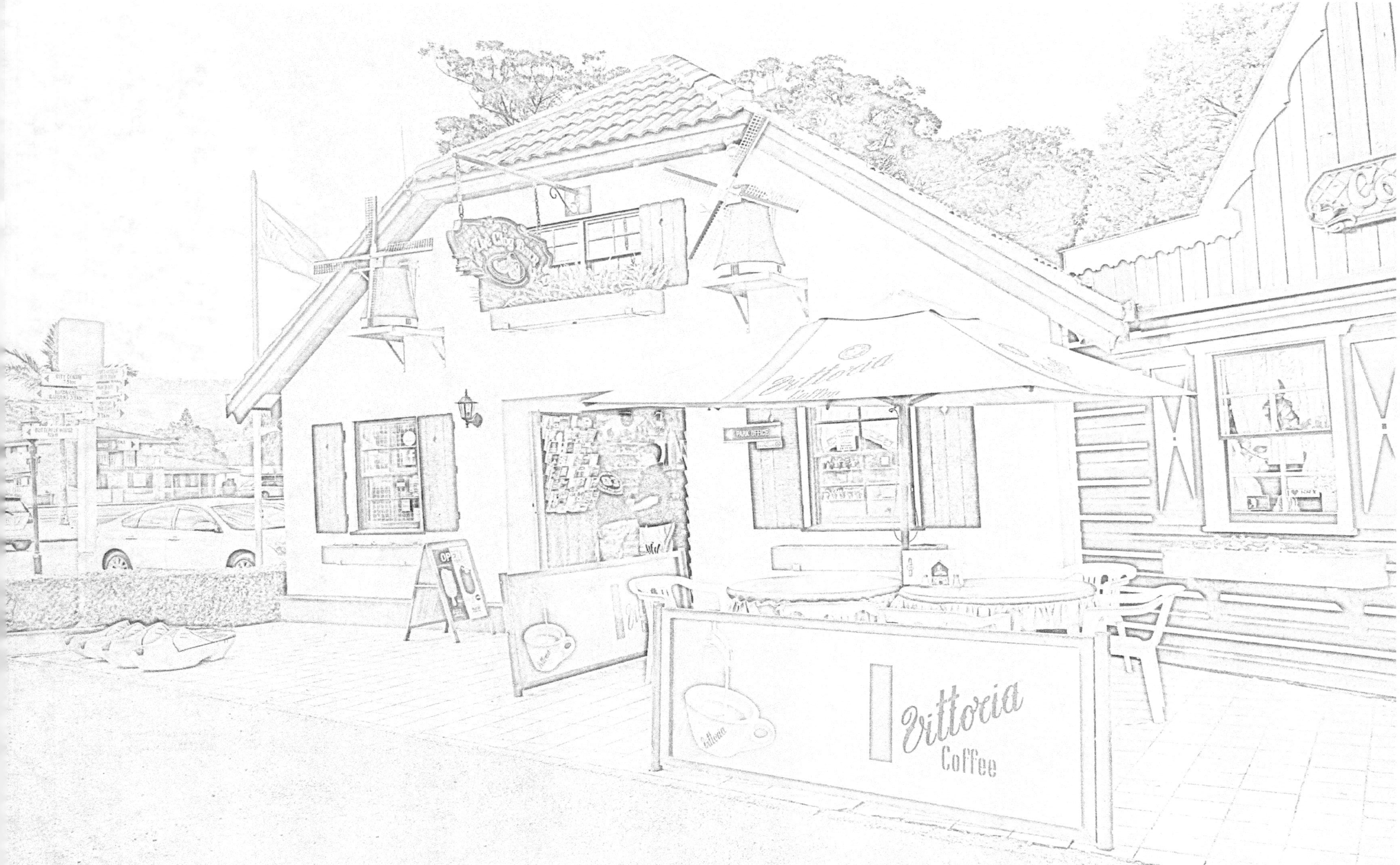
Vittoria
Coffee
PARK OFFICE

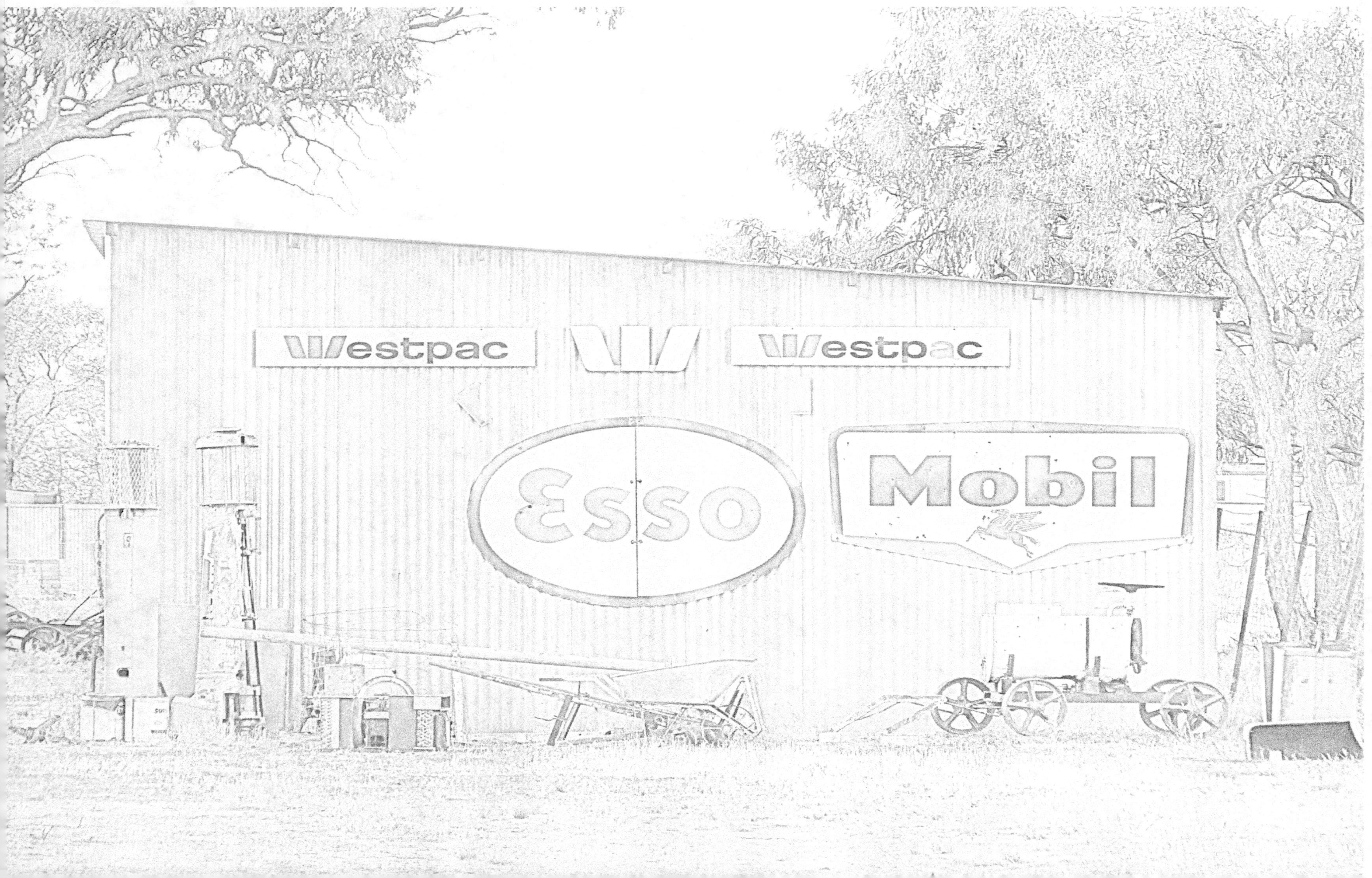
Westpac
Westpac
Esso
Mobil

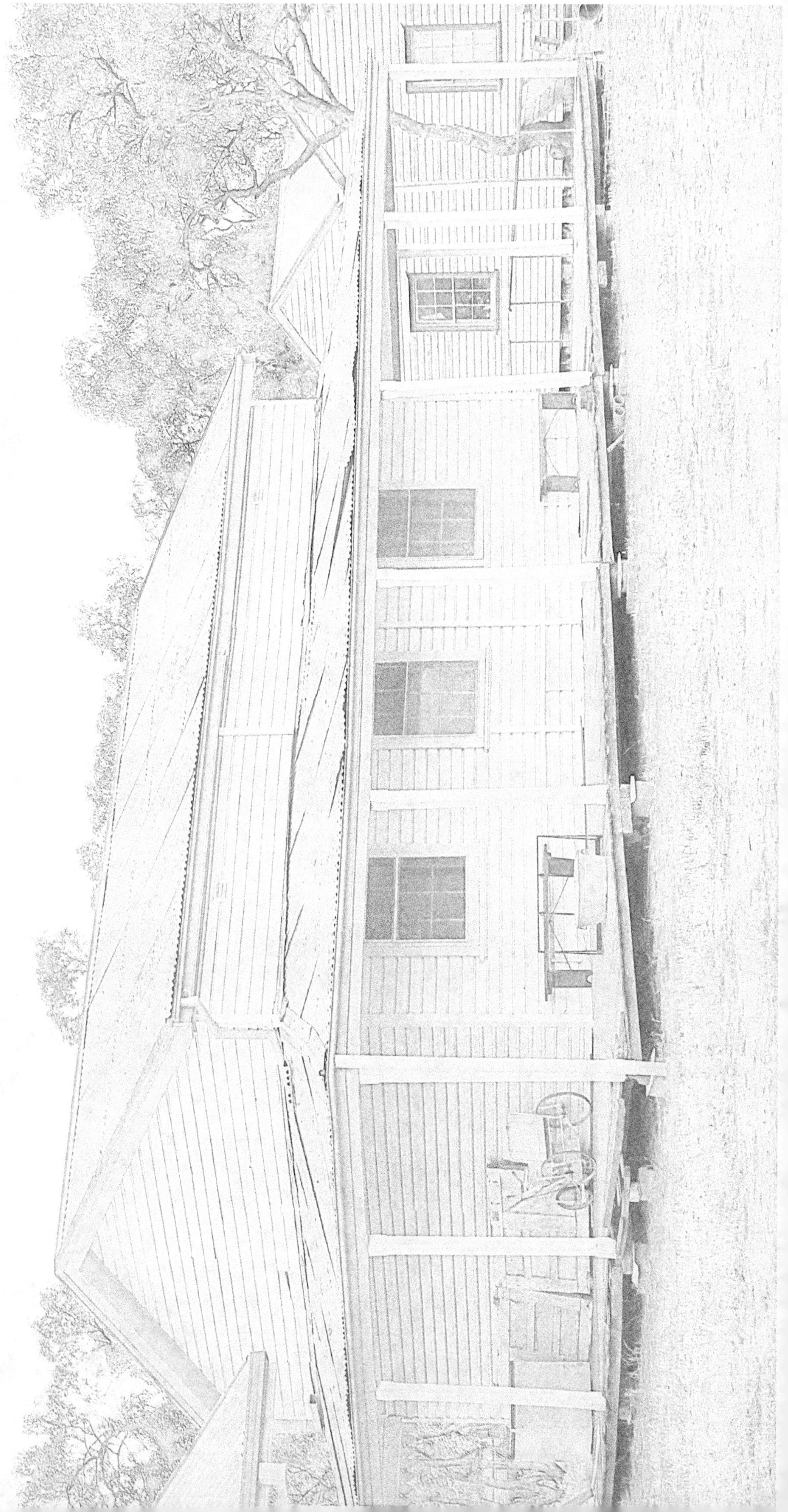

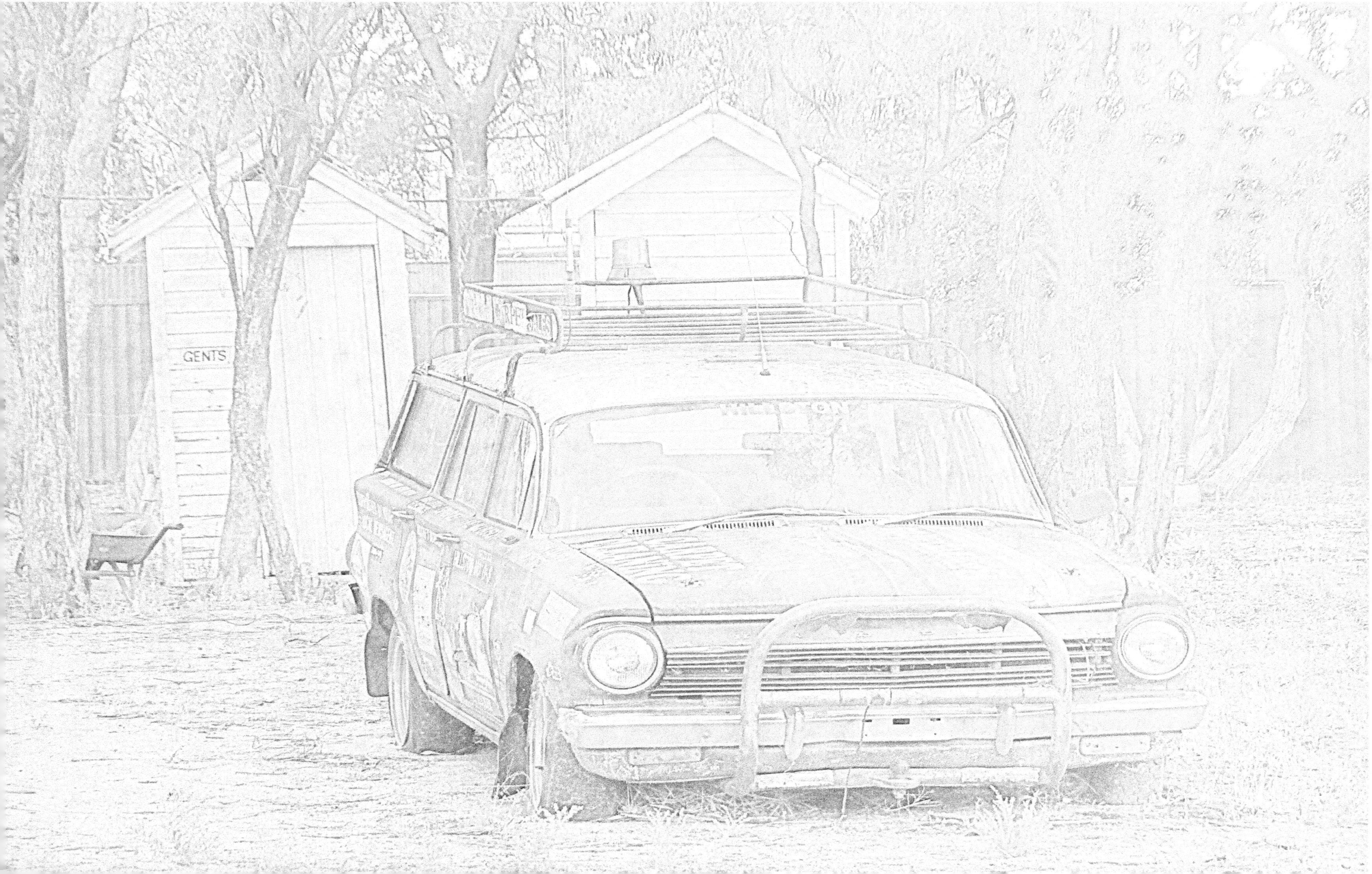
GENTS

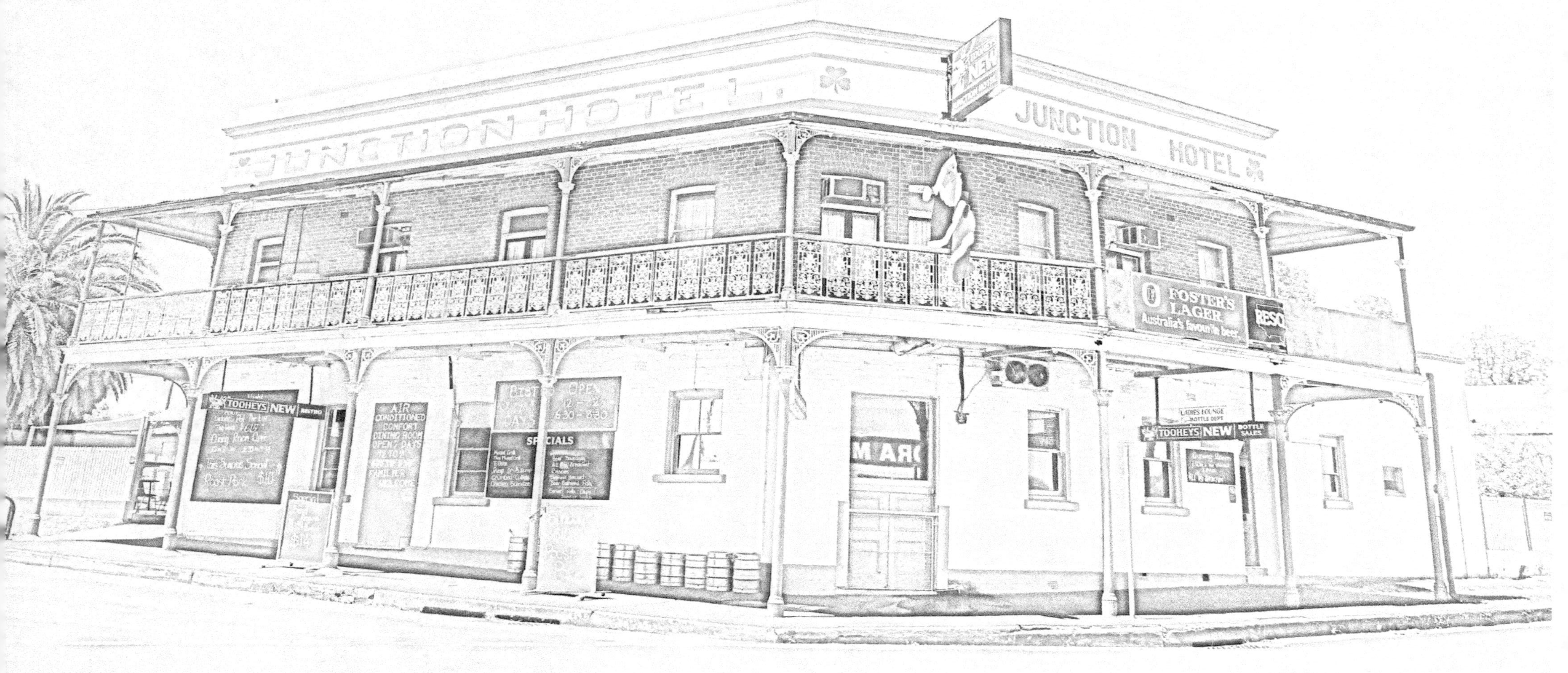
JUNCTION HOTEL
JUNCTION HOTEL
TOOHEYS NEW
FOSTER'S LAGER
Australia's favourite beer
TOOHEYS NEW BISTRO
AIR CONDITIONED COMFORT DINING ROOM OPEN 7 DAYS
SPECIALS
LADIES LOUNGE
BOTTLE DEPT
TOOHEYS NEW BOTTLE SALES

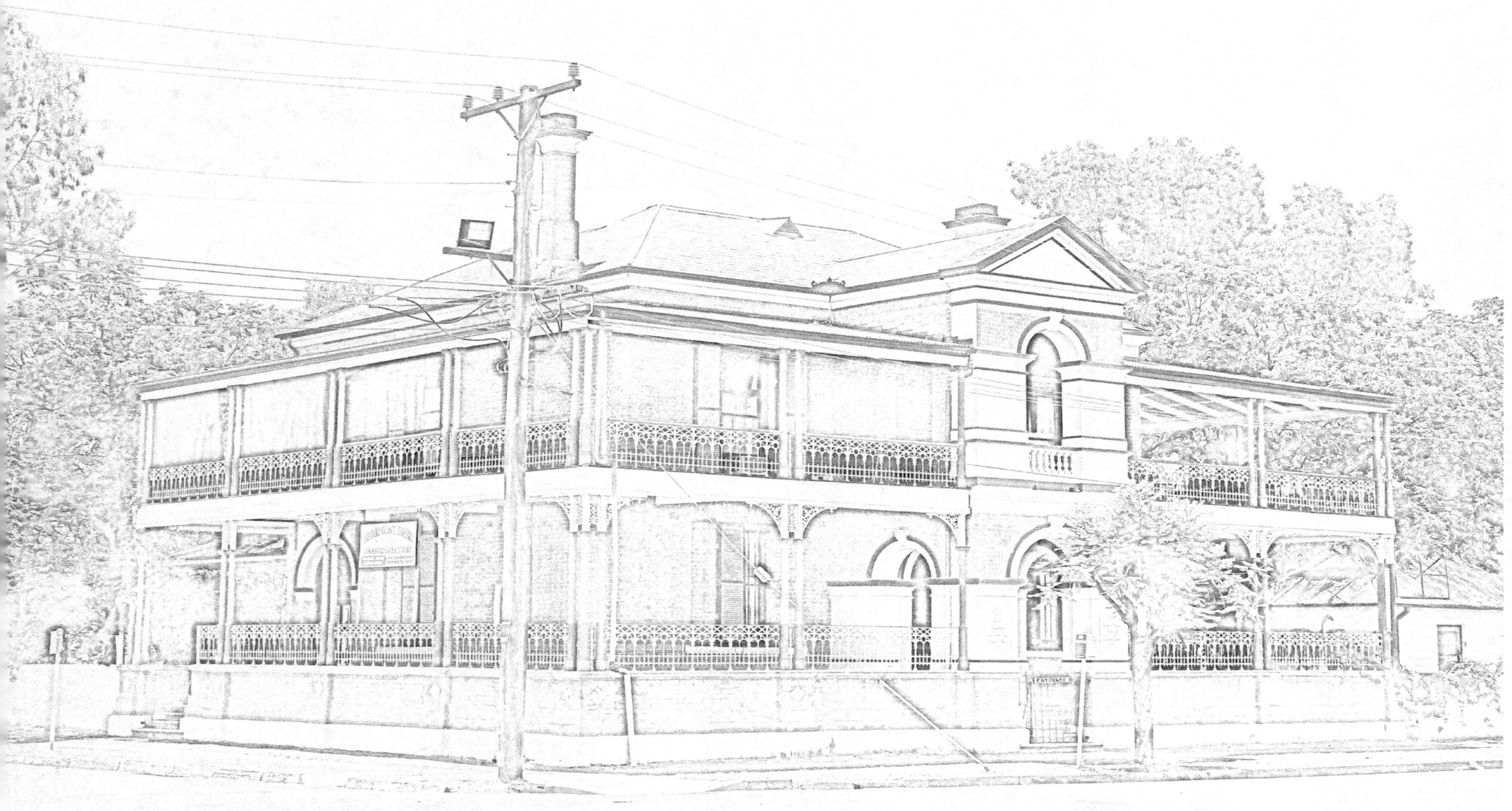

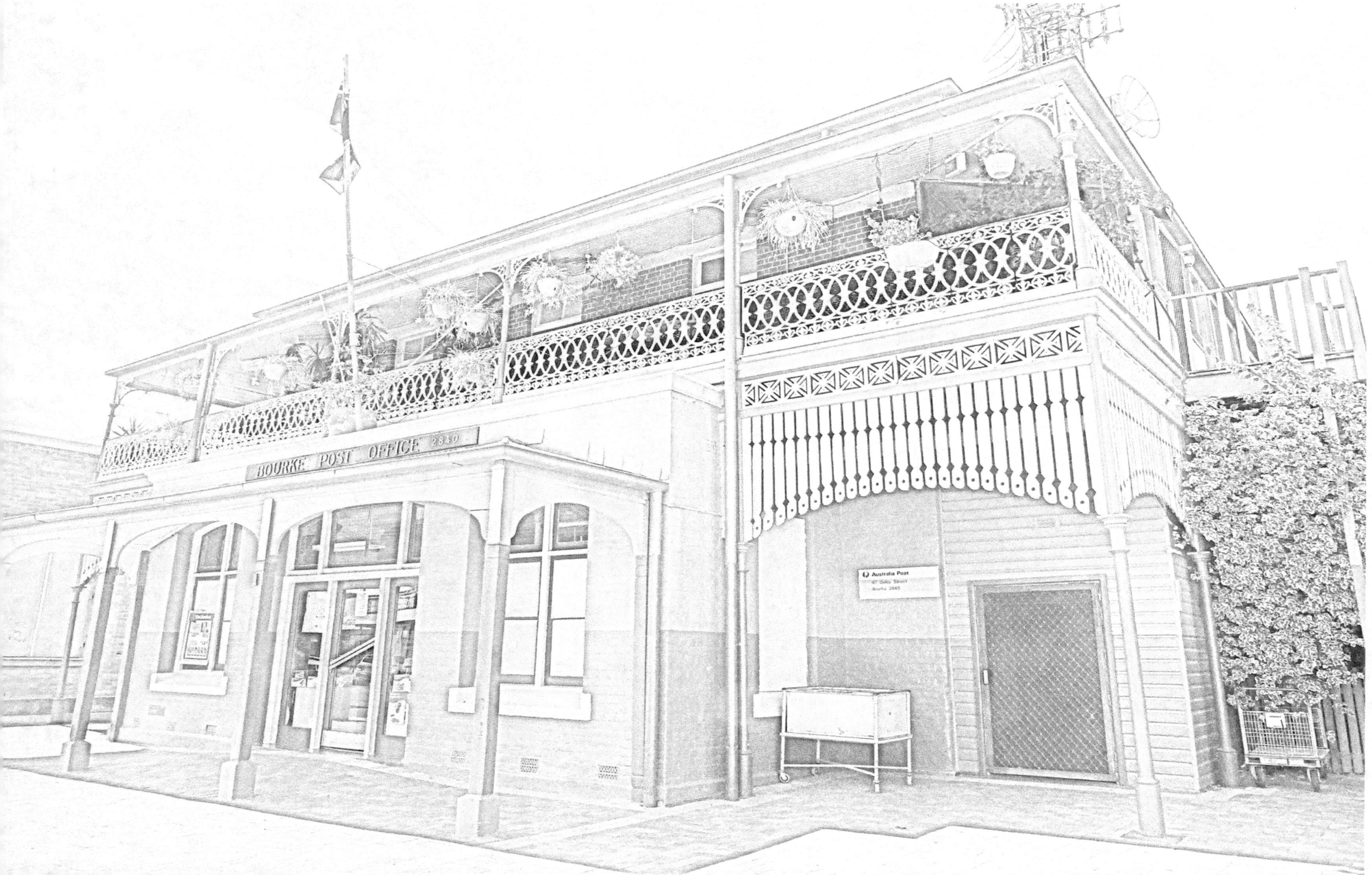
BOURKE POST OFFICE 2840
Australia Post

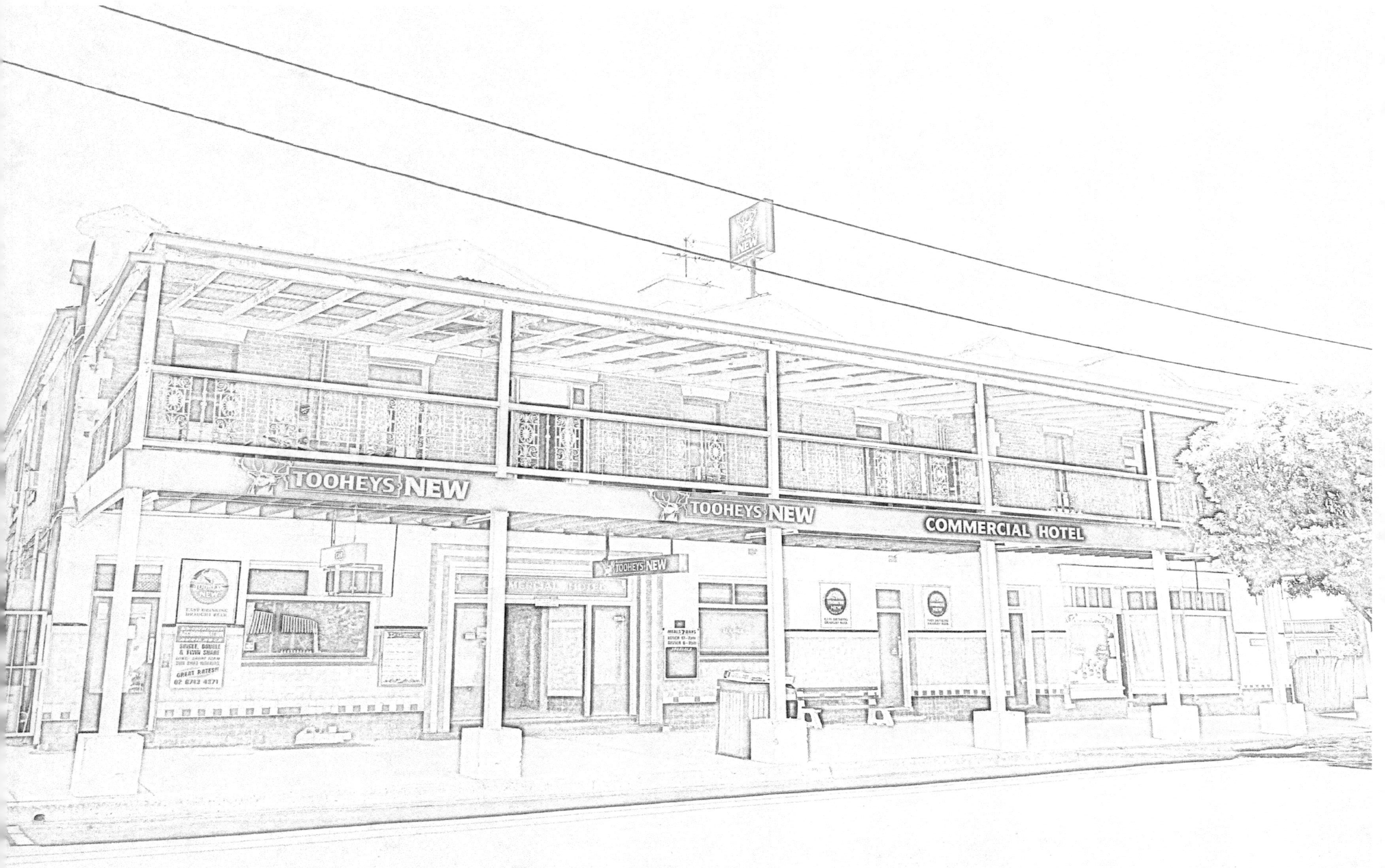
TOOHEYS NEW
TOOHEYS NEW
COMMERCIAL HOTEL
TOOHEYS NEW
SINGLE, DOUBLE & TWIN SHARE
GREAT RATES!!
02 6742 4371
MEALS 7 DAYS

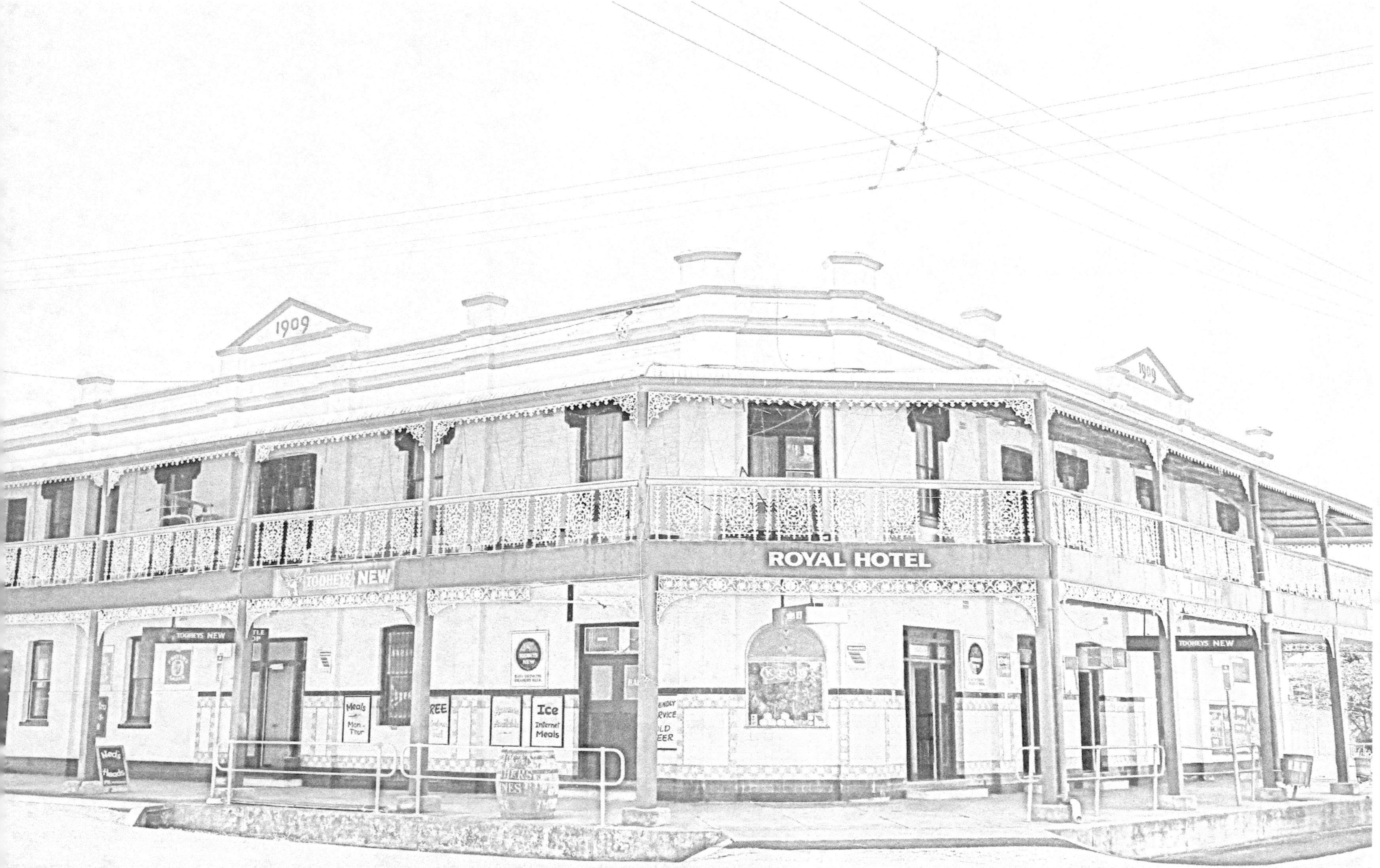
1909
ROYAL HOTEL
TOOHEYS NEW
TOOHEYS NEW
TOOHEYS NEW
1909
Meals
Mon - Thur
Ice
Internet
Meals

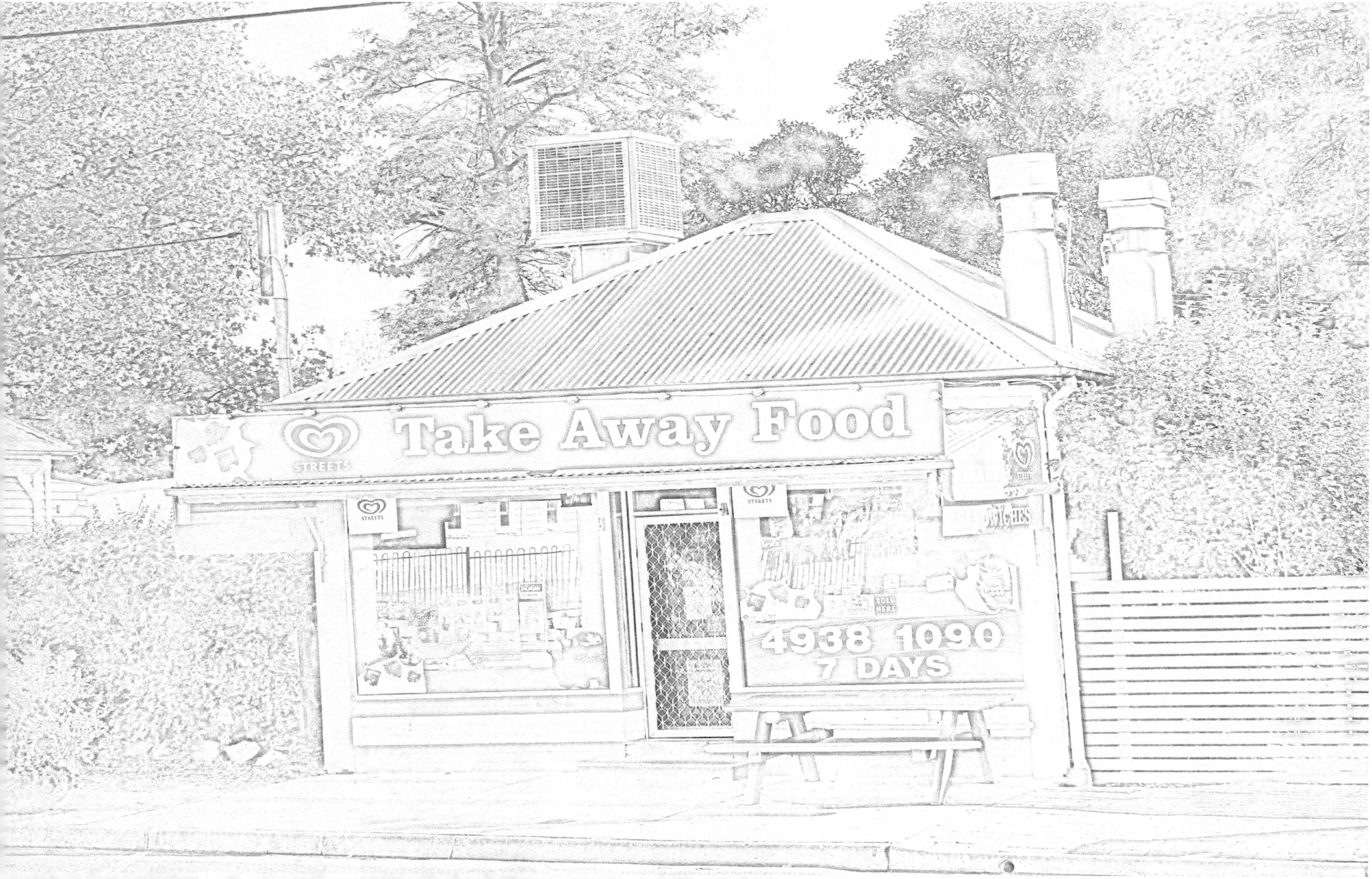
STREETS
Take Away Food
STREETS
STREETS
4938 1090
7 DAYS

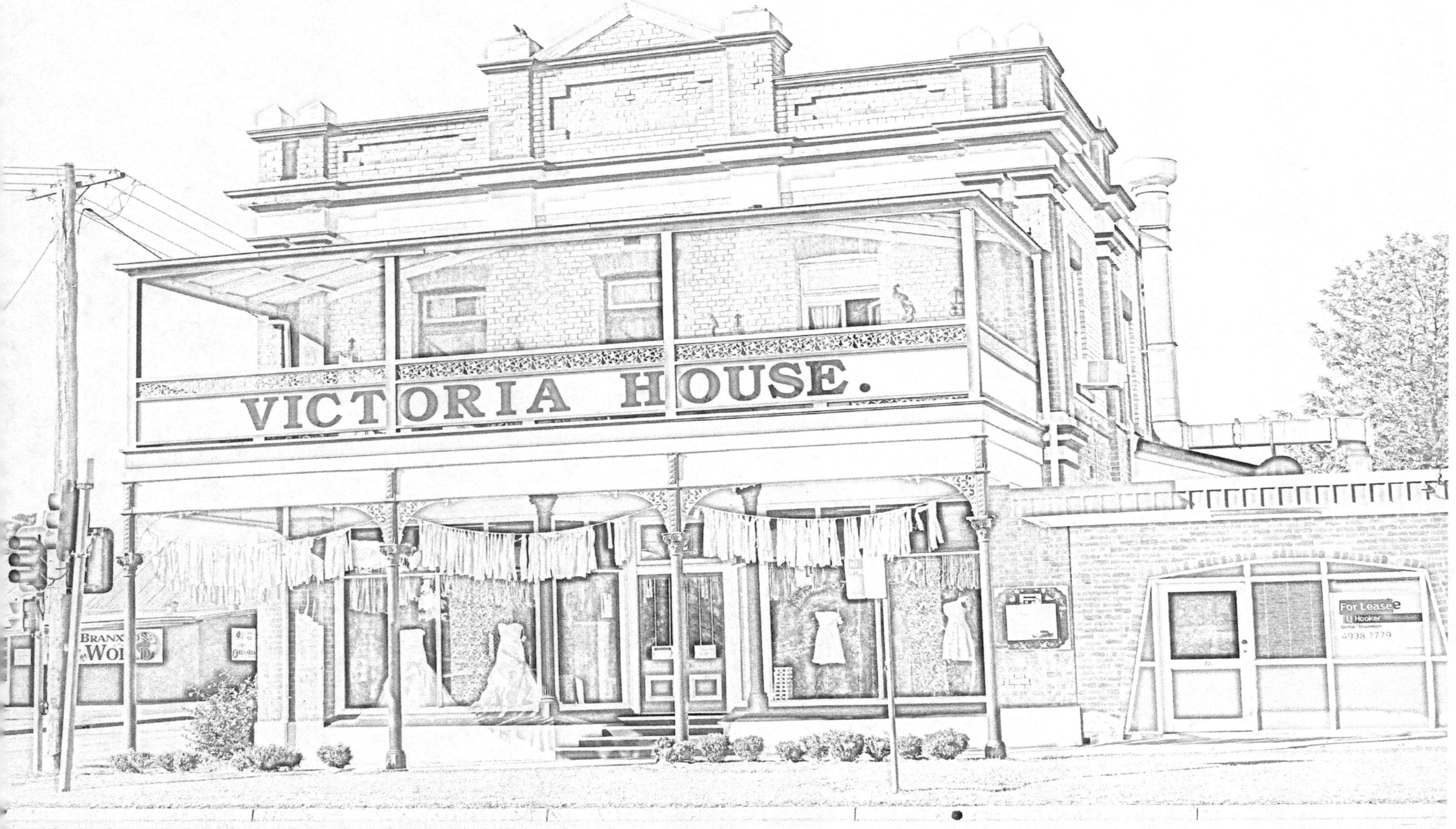
VICTORIA HOUSE.
For Lease
LJ Hooker
4938 7779

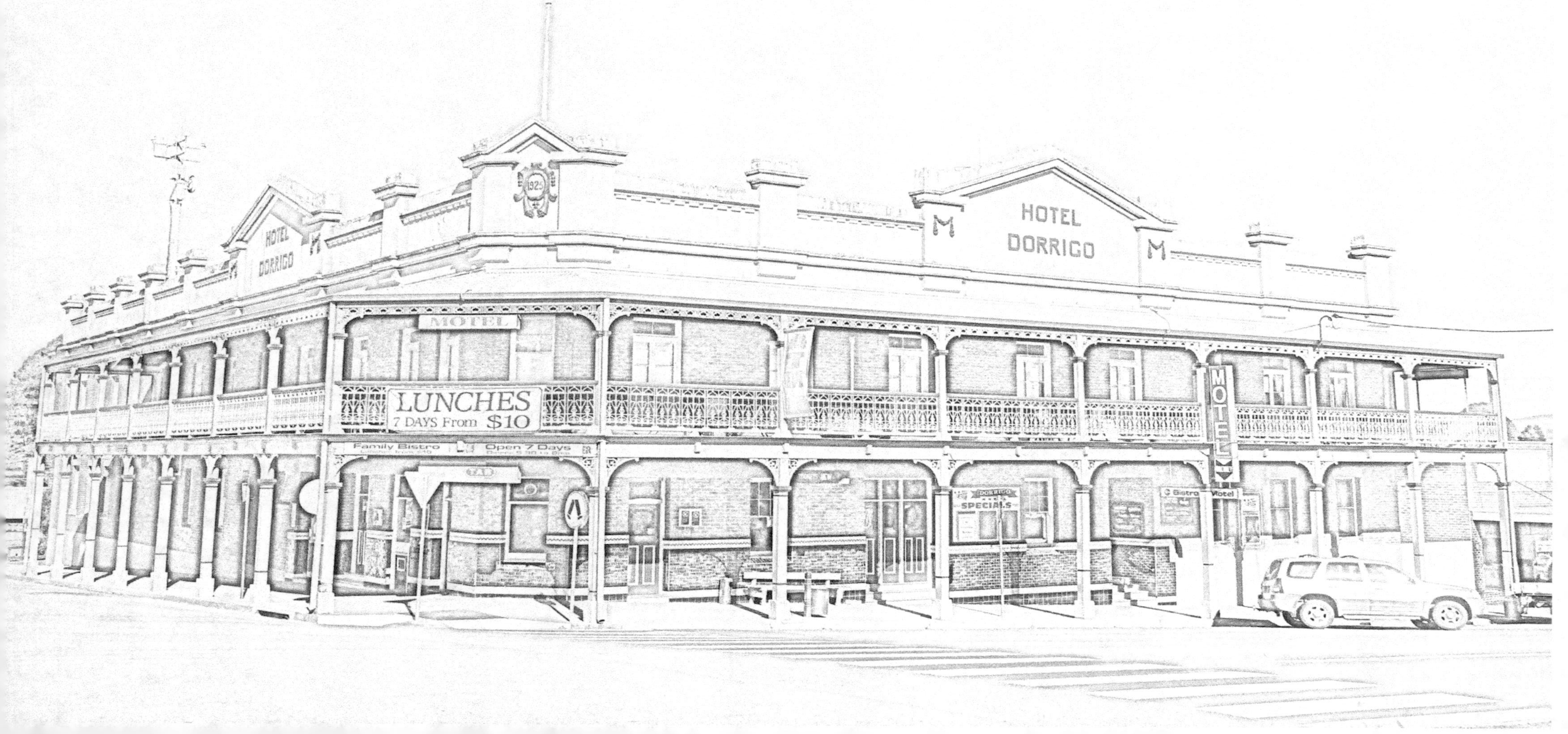
HOTEL DORRICO
1925
HOTEL DORRICO
MOTEL
LUNCHES
7 DAYS From $10
Family Bistro
Open 7 Days
MOTEL
DORRIGO
SPECIALS
Bistro
Motel

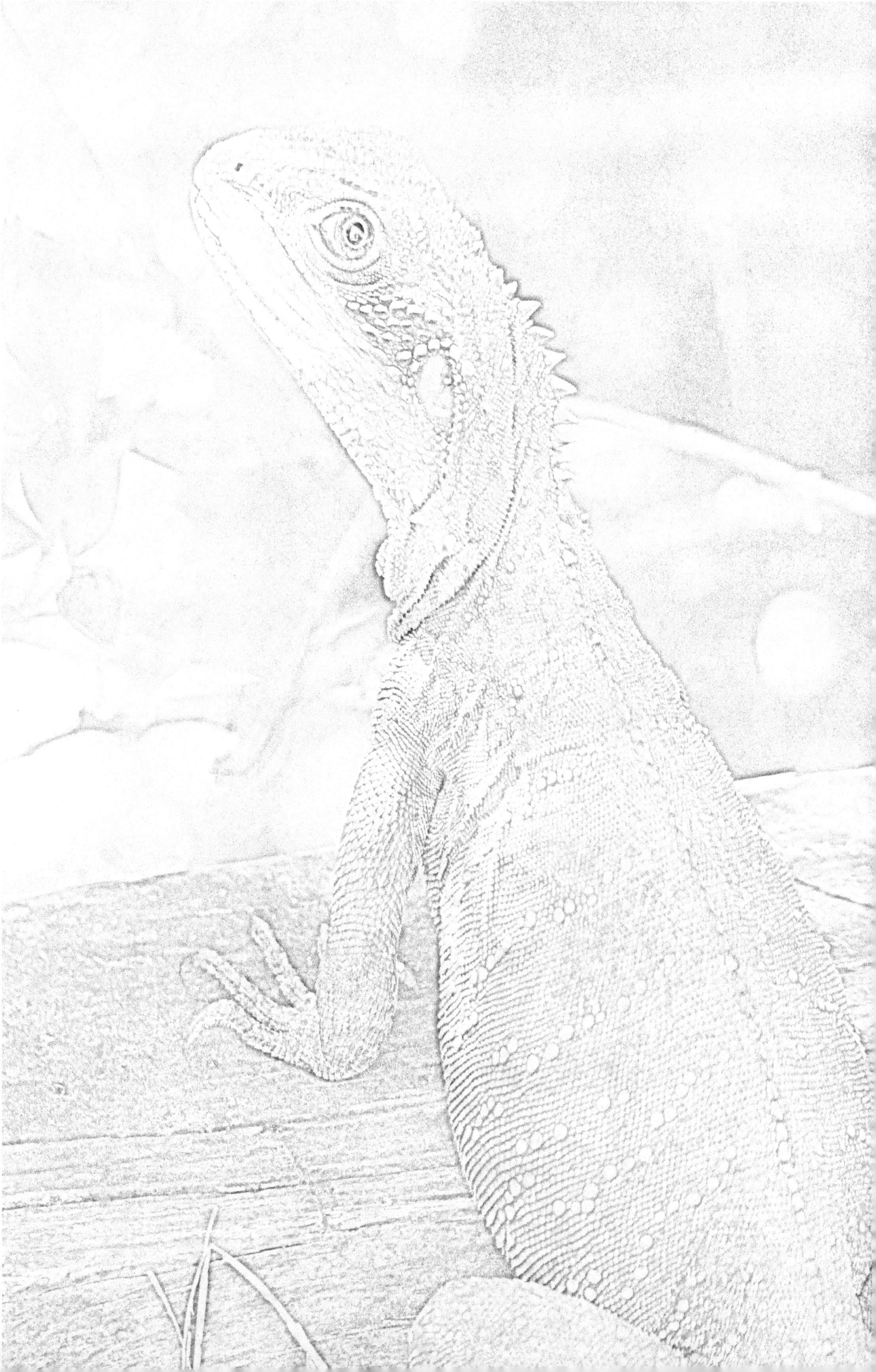

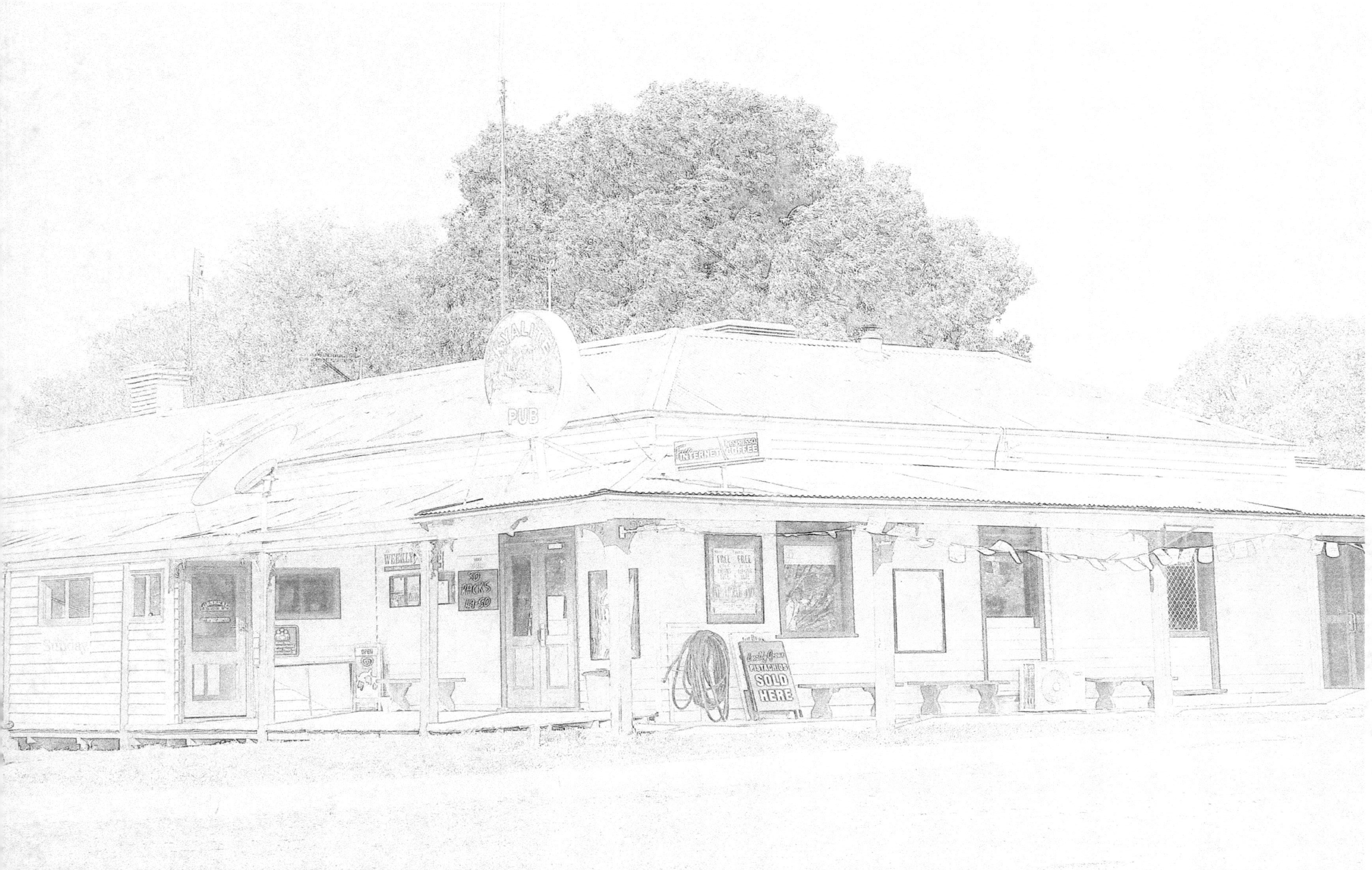

PUB
INTERNET
COFFEE
WEEKLY
30 PACKS 49.50
FREE FREE
PISTACHIOS
SOLD HERE
OPEN

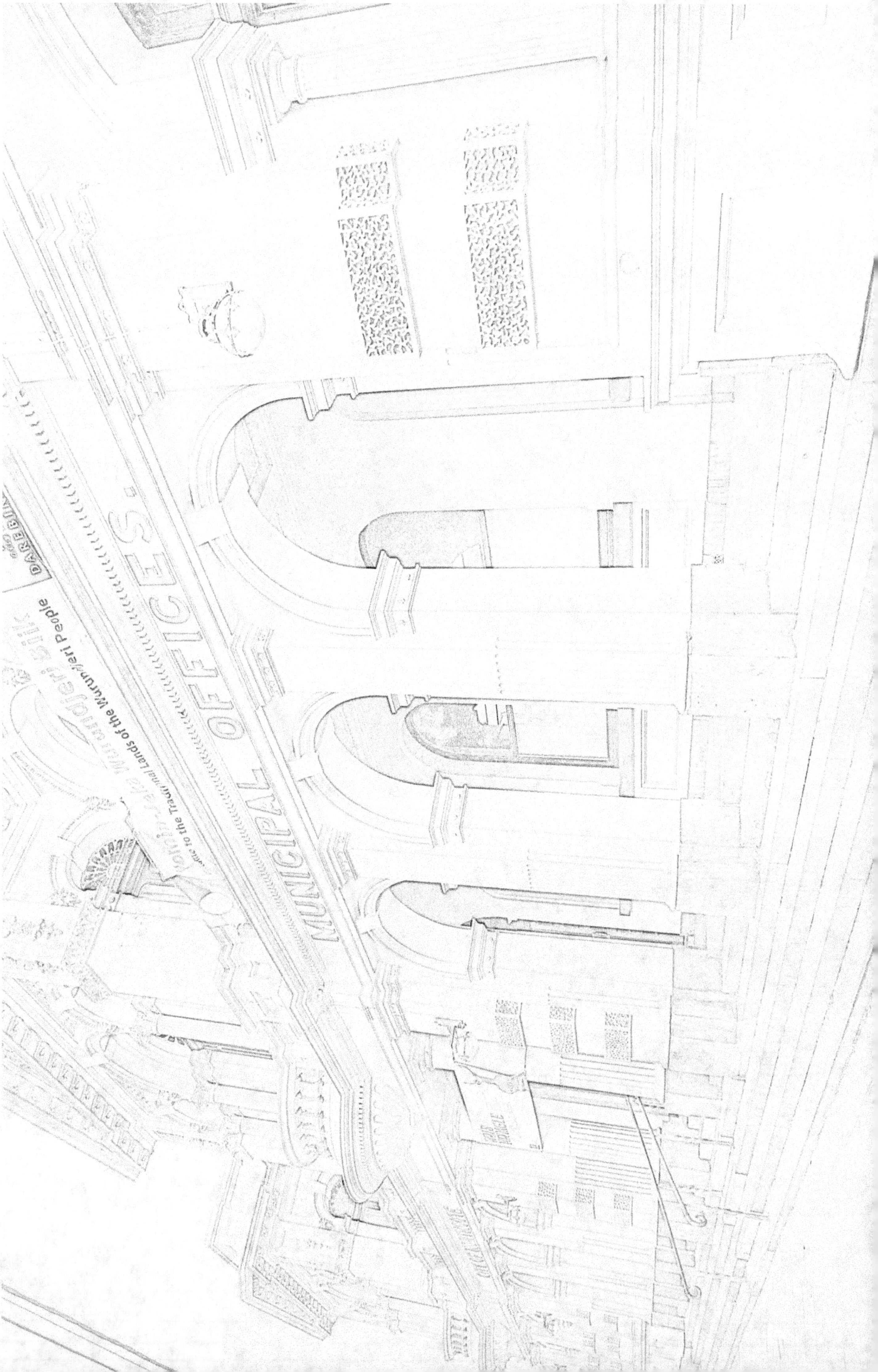
MUNICIPAL OFFICES
to the Traditional Lands of the Wurundjeri People

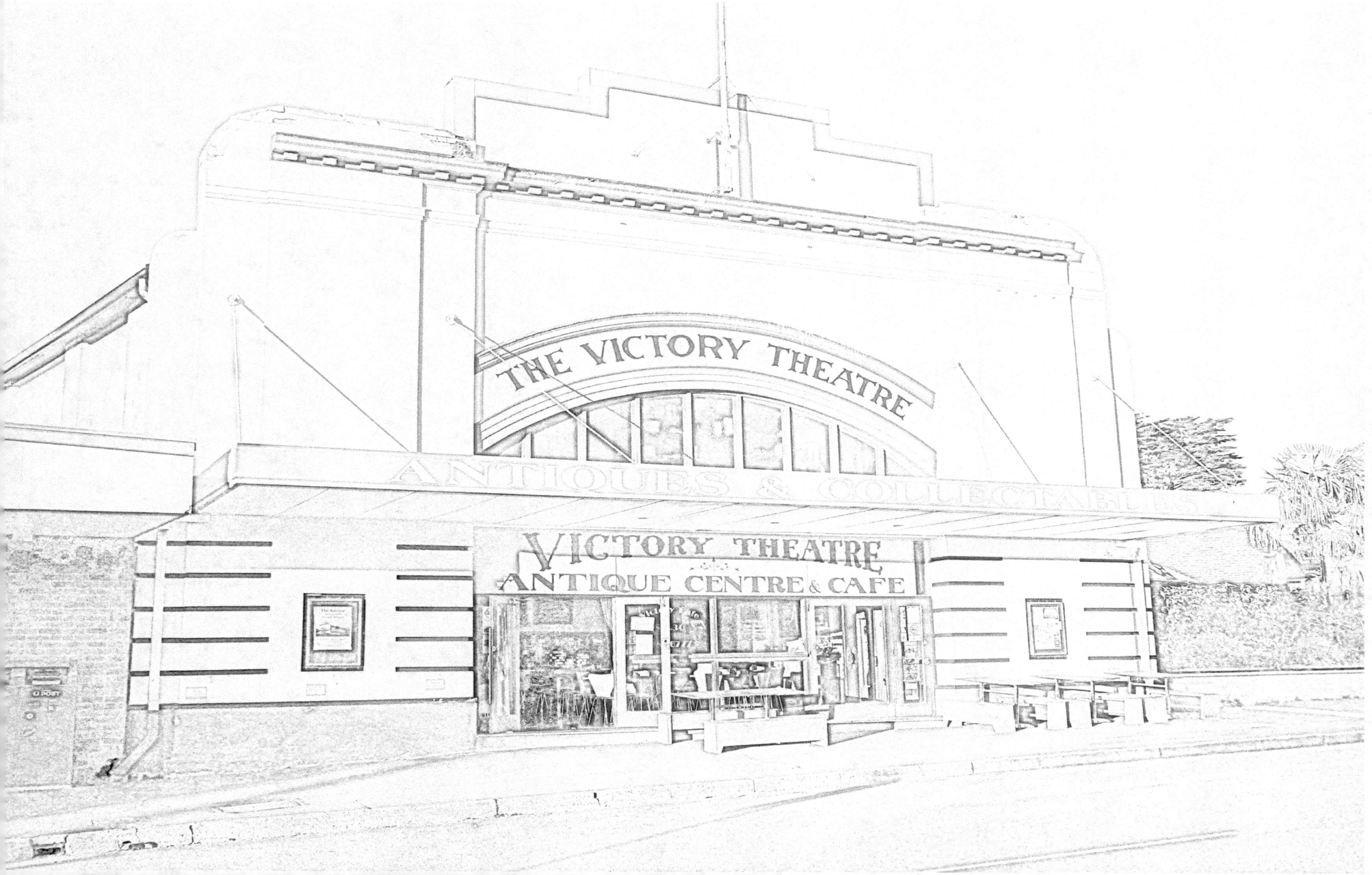
THE VICTORY THEATRE
ANTIQUES & COLLECTABLES
VICTORY THEATRE
ANTIQUE CENTRE & CAFE
POST

www.ingramcontent.com/pod-product-compliance
Lightning Source LLC
Chambersburg PA
CBHW081049180526
45170CB00005B/1739